28 Thoughts On Digital Revolution

The good, the bad and the ugly personality traits of our digitally enhanced world

JONATHAN MACDONALD

ISBN-13: 978-1495463471

ISBN-10: 1495463478

jonathanmacdonald.com

CONTENTS

INTRODUCTION

28 Thoughts On Digital Revolution is a collection of thoughts I developed between 2006 and 2014 with regards to the digital revolution we are living in.

I developed them with the intention of expanding thought within others and enabling positive action. I did this because every aspect of life and business has been fundamentally affected by the paradigm shift from industrial technology to the consumerised, digital technology that now outnumbers the human population.

The 28 thoughts in this collection originally amounted to over 5000 blog posts and speeches. In my head they didn't present themselves in any particular order, although I feel they fall into distinct categories.

There are observations I've made during the years of working deep within and alongside many organisations, large and small. There are technology thoughts that address the sometimes hidden aspects of the fascinating tools we now have at our disposal. I address privacy as a concept after this, which is linked to my thinking on big data. My thoughts about online safety follow afterward, before looking at positive opportunities in advocacy and loyalty. Towards the end you'll find my perspective on the topic of citizenship and finally, a range of random ideas I've had over the years, which are linked directly to the trends and developments I've witnessed and predicted for the future.

Within all of this, I hope you find something of value.

Jonathan MacDonald

PART ONE: OBSERVATIONS

1. CHANGE IS THE ENEMY OF THE COMPETENT – a thought on how we deal with change

A long time ago when I started helping companies interpret how to use the Internet I was met with a significant level of negativity.

During my tenure as the Chairman of the retail side of the British Music Industry, one particular retailer who thought that I was "representing the Internet" said that he would make sure I was "shut down".

Years later I was laughed at in boardrooms when explaining to supermarkets they could sell groceries online.

After this I was kicked out of meetings for talking about the virtualisation of physical products and services.

Within the last six years I've been taken aside and quietly told that I have no right to talk about "digital black magic" to serious businessmen. Told instead to "bring back proof and case studies to show how markets had been re-defined online".

At the time though, no case studies existed and the only proof we had was from Cern, considered to be unrelated to commerciality by many organisations.

As I cut my teeth as a private adviser I was invited by the Government to discuss how the effect of the web could be "slowed down".

In February 2006 when I announced the forthcoming trend in permission mobile marketing, I was cornered in a corridor by two very angry traditional advertising guys who were absolutely furious that I was "rocking the boat".

Over my entire career I've faced these reactions. I'm used to it.

You can't win against them by arguing back. You can't win by entering into long debates. To some people the existence of absolute undisputable evidence is the only thing they will accept – but actually that's not it. I've realised that their issue is not the actual issue.

The fact is, change is the enemy of the competent as it re-defines the safe place within which the competent dwell.

The competent cannot stand change. Ultimately it makes them scared as what they think they know is being challenged.

If anything changes, the only way they feel comfortable is if they can pragmatically re-design the walls of their safe place, at their speed and within their level of understanding, without rocking any boats.

However change doesn't wait for that, hence being so unattractive. Change is persistent and unrelenting in the face of those who resist.

As the Chinese proverb says: "When the winds of change are blowing, some build a shelter, others build a windmill."

I'm in the windmill business. Are you?

2. INTERNAL VS. EXTERNAL PURPOSE – a thought on making sense inside and outside a company

When setting out on a mission to innovate, grow and change, it is imperative to start with a purpose.

This shouldn't be an internal purpose like increasing sales; this should be an external purpose like building a particular customer service or something else that is directly linked to value creation for humans. Sales are great it's just that nobody outside your organisation cares.

An internal purpose (like sales for example), de-prioritises value to anyone outside the organisation. External purpose (like human value for example) is about what can be created for others. And therein lies the magic.

I have noticed that even the most business-like professionals find it far more rewarding and relaxing to drop the internal mandates and start thinking human value. Sometimes it takes a while to shift the mind but once shifted, the flow usually starts with abundance.

Mostly this happens against organisational governance, but the perspective of "what business we are actually in" becomes clearer than ever before and the resulting ideas become more viable for citizen engagement to happen.

In almost all cases it is this approach that drives sales rather than a campaign with only selfish intent.

It's a great thing to experience and is rock solid in terms of logic in an ultra-connected world. They win so you win. Not the other way around. Enjoy the ride.

3. WHAT LIES BENEATH – a thought on the relative accuracy of information, statistics and misrepresentation

Recently, Fast Company published an article relating to a new study from Princeton's Department of Mechanical and Aerospace Engineering, claiming that "Facebook will lose 80% of users by 2017"[1]. This article was duly shared around the world across multiple channels, reaching millions of people. If you looked very carefully though, you'd find that the statistics are exclusively based on how many times the word 'Facebook' appears in Google analytics. Critically, these analytics do not include mobile usage, which accounts for the majority of Internet traffic, including a rise to over 100 million Facebook users. Such insight was quietly set aside to make way for the attention-grabbing headline.

We see many market reports and professional comment that, one would assume, is valid and considered. However, I see a continuous trend where hidden information resides behind colourful charts that are widely quoted and used as a basis for investment of time, energy or money. In the Black Swan, Taleb calls this 'silent evidence'[2]. Are we seeing the full picture? It may be circumstance that determines the answer. After all, sub-editors often remove the subtleties that surround what is written. Obviously, our consumption of information has to be made to fit our increasingly 'bite-size' and 'instant satisfaction' personalities, but I fear this may be at the expense of real truth.

In its most basic form, silent evidence is easy to spot. For example, if I were to prove to you that sober drivers cause more accidents than drivers under the influence of alcohol, would you conclude that it is safer to drive whilst under the influence?

That seems to be presented in my argument, however what is missing is that there are a relatively small number of drivers who drive under the influence, but who account for a disproportionately high number of accidents.

This trap is actually very common. As it happens, there are a number of ways in which information can be misleading, including:

- *False data* - an easy one, just plain downright lies
- *Bad sampling* - often seen where a very small segment of people are asked a question and the resulting percentages are scaled across a much larger population
- *Predictive questions* - a modern day media classic is "would you like adverts on your mobile device?" This is predominantly asked when the required result is a resounding 'no'. If you want the answer to include more 'yes' responses, you would remove the word advertising and switch it for "useful content that would make your life better?" This leads to a major skew towards the positive. Either way, the questions have predictable answers
- *Misleading selections* - commonly where a snapshot of real data is used which intentionally misses out preceding periods which would harm the impact – for instance, if you wanted to show an upturn in advertising spend, but only three months in a year had an increase, you wouldn't show the downturn that happened before, only the growing months (which may well be making up a fraction of the previous loss)
- *Self-adjusted rankings* - with the editorial right to remove justification of ranking. In whatever industry you're in, you may have seen companies who claim to be the "World's Number 1". Surely there can only be one, right? But from closer inspection you find that the information not included is the part that defines exactly what ranking conditions they include. Is it in terms of revenue, profit, employee numbers or

experience of the CEO? We are only shown the juicy bits and the terms and conditions are nowhere to be seen

- *Limiting qualifiers* - one of my favourites and similar to self-adjusted rankings. This is where you word a statistic in a way that the result is essentially fixed. For instance: "The brown bear is the largest land predator in the world". The word 'predator' rules out elephants which are bigger but aren't predators, while the word 'land' rules out various whales which are predators but don't live on land. The statement is built for the brown bear to dominate
- *Percentage accentuation* - so common. Take a company making a bunch of people redundant. If the company has 100 staff and gets rid of 20, in the interests of making the statistic sexier, it would be "Company lays off 20% of entire workforce!" because 20 people doesn't sound anywhere near as dramatic as 20%. However, in a company of 1 million, the 20% is still quite sexy but nothing sounds as big as "Company lays off 200,000 people!" The liberal insertion of exclamation marks is my own of course…

In summary, as publishers we have a responsibility to promote accurate and contextually detailed data to others, and as viewers, a responsibility to dig deeper. As information spreads so quickly in this ultra-connected world, the misrepresentation of truth re-frames what 'truth' is – especially when those in a position of authority are relaying information that is believed on sight.

To quote an unknown source discussing statistics:

"86% of statistics are made up on the spot and the remaining 24% are mathematically flawed."

Spot on.

4. THE HIDDEN TRUTH OF SOCIAL MEDIA – a thought on the realities of social media

When a new invention comes along it is natural that we look for something tangible to which we can attach ourselves. Learning a new subject is much harder if we don't bring it down to a real level. You may recognise this in learning a new language, where the methods often include real-life scenarios in which, for example, someone is asking for directions or ordering a coffee. In my French lessons that person was always called Thierry and he had some strange fascination with locating the library… but that's not important right now.

As technology became more affordable and was able to do more, the amount we interacted with each other, and the volume of content involved, increased exponentially. The channels within which we interacted became an attractive proposition for media companies who published content for people to consume (e.g. newspapers), retailers who displayed items for sale (e.g. traditional shops that went online), and of course advertisers who wanted to encourage people to buy products and services.

Over the last 100 years or so these media channels were named and in due course the most recent opportunity took its name as 'Social Media': Lots of social interactions = big media opportunity.

One by one the industries started to create Social Media strategies that, unsurprisingly, were based on adjusting their other channel strategies to take into account the nuances of this new format. This wasn't in terms of simply putting a TV ad on Facebook; it was in terms of viewing people who were privately interacting on Social Media as a passive audience as they were when watching TV.

In short, the primary focus on Social Media was originally through a fixed lens of marketing communications campaigns, and I'm here to report this is still the case in most circumstances.

It is tempting for companies to look at the Social Media landscape through this fixed lens of campaigns and start with a channel perspective. In other words:

"What can we do with an app to promote our brand in this campaign?"

"What platform can we build so people engage with us?"

"What is technically possible so people can buy from us using digital?"

However there are two major considerations that place this viewpoint under extreme question:

1. The world of Social Media opportunities is a minor part of what is actually happening in society and business. The fundamental increase in the power that people have, manifesting often as the ability for anyone (authorised or not) to create, edit, publish and share, means that whether we like it or not, whatever an organisation delivers into the public domain can be instantly adjusted, published and promoted. This removes the traditional levels of control and predictability a company once had over how people were likely going to think and behave. This affects the entire value chain… every single aspect of doing business. In plain English – whatever you think you controlled is now, at best, in shared control with the outside world who don't have any of your corporate guidance or governance.

2. The opportunities in Social Media are likely to be under-exploited due to the misinterpretation of Social Media. Having a fixed lens of marketing communications and/or a priority of tool, platform or channel, means that the above reality is unlikely to be properly considered for what is in reality a revolution-sized paradigm shift that impacts the entire value chain. Again, in plain English – if you want to benefit from the changes around us it is unlikely that a biased and limited perspective will produce the results you and your stakeholders are expecting.

What validates these points?

The media is fundamentally different from what we've known before. The traditional media landscape was one of owned or bought media (i.e. on a site, in a film, on a page, in a search result or on a TV show). The new landscape is one of earned media, which is within recommendation and within conversation. This earned media space runs on a different language from traditional media and that's a language of passion and belief. In simple terms – what people care about and what matters to their lives.

Earned media isn't something that can be bought, it can only be earned. The ways of earning the opportunity can only come from the ways humans earn belief and trust from each other. Typically this starts from positive interactions, then into consistency, developing credibility, authenticity, then finally trust and (the holy grail) loyalty.

There is empirical evidence of this, not only from the science of how we interact as humans, but also in the mixed fortunes you see around you today. You'll notice the companies who haven't understood earned media as when something goes wrong for them in public, nobody sticks up for them – let alone their declining profits and increased concern from analysts in the City. Tesco is one example[3]. Industry experts and the company itself claim that changes in consumer behaviour are to blame… yet the reality is far deeper and the behavioural aspect is just one dimension of the paradigm shift.

Elsewhere you'll notice companies who have understood this paradigm because their marketing function, defence mechanism, and sales force aren't necessarily people who are paid by the company directly. No, these are people who believe. Adjacent to this belief are sales and profit boosts.

Muji is a fine example of this, although commentators talk of Lego more commonly[4]. Industry experts and the company itself claim that new product lines are the reason… yet, again, the reality is far deeper and releasing new product lines is the tip of an iceberg that runs through a wider strategy of direct and calculated citizen involvement[5].

If you're interested you can find dozens of other case studies and examples in this paper I co-authored with Liri Andersson at this fluid world: http://thisfluidworld.com/branddemocratisation.pdf

What can be done about it?

How can we undo the terminology and mindset that have created this Social Media beast that drives massive valuations and numerous headlines? How can we reverse the effects and un-hire the heads of social, heads of digital and heads of mobile? Should we even attempt to change course? After all, we've made the investments and now we eagerly await the returns that seem to always be a 'maybe next year' promise.

The practical advice would be this:

Take immediate action in fully understanding what's really going on and what it means to you in your life and to your company – from the drivers of change to the science of earned media. Not through a biased lens of any particular channel or discipline. Not from the perspective of a partner company who need you to think in a certain way so you buy more from them, but from an agnostic external perspective.

You can only make powerful decisions and devise relevant strategies from truly understanding what's happening.

After pondering on this for a long time and experiencing many companies over recent years misinterpreting Social Media (and related tools, platforms and channels), I've realised two things:

1. It's only natural that this new concept should adopt the existing mindset. Who knew the tide itself had changed? All we saw was that a new media emerged with lots of eyeballs to market to – little did anyone know that the playing field had been monumentally re-constructed.

2. Eventual failure will provide the realisation. The only convincer for those who question the above logic will be failure from misinterpretation and malpractice. I don't mean this to sound combative. I genuinely feel that under-performance against objective or expectation will speak for itself. Whilst the digital 'gurus' and marketing 'experts' promise the moon, the financiers expect results, and in a capitalist world, the results need to be delivered. But the money is only one side.

As for the people, we in the public expect honesty and openness. We expect companies to have the same values as humans. The results we'd like are for a company to stand for something we can believe in, and truly mean it in everything they do (rather than just everything they say). When any of these results don't appear (or when a competitor does interpret the seismic changes appropriately), the fall-out will separate the competition in the natural order of evolution.

5. PERSONAL ECHONOMICS – a thought on how we are affected by the actions and opinions of others

We humans have a tendency to judge ourselves upon the feedback from others. This peer validation can be super important, especially in situations where it is vital that the other party accepts or admires you.

For example, if you are interviewing for a job you really want, it's very useful to know what you could be doing better, or what has resonated most. In personal relationships the same applies of course. Building something that works requires both parties to feel as if they are being valued.

Then, as we monitor reactions and pick up on clues that portray how we are being received, it's natural for us to try and change things in our own behaviour that may improve things. It's as if we are putting stuff out and listening to the echo back, adjusting as we go.

This is not news; we're social animals and the desire to fit into our social environment is a principal part of our humanity. However, is it possible to change how we are to such an extent we surrender being our true selves?

We rapidly run in to a question of whether the changes we make are designing new versions of ourselves that are decreasingly linked to our core? Or is it as Perry Farrell from Jane's Addiction said: "You never really change like they say, you only become more like yourself."[6]

Either way, it would seem our deep desire to be accepted has an impact on who we are and that makes me wonder about whether that is always such a good thing.

On one hand it is imperative for the non-pathological to fit into society, but on the other I'd argue it's also desirable to discover who you are and be true to it – but not at any expense though, there's a balance to be set. In my mind I call this balancing of echoes 'Echonomics'.

Within the balance I think we need a filter that enables us to somehow decide who we would amend what for. I observe many instances of people who have developed behaviours to fit in with situations that they don't find particularly valuable. I have seen people (myself included) going through the motions to match expectations of others where there is no shred of mutual respect.

I fear that this behaviour is chipping away internally, leaving small scratches and sometimes, large scars. Any 'sensible' person would determine who would be deserving of self-change, but sometimes other factors override our common sense and layer on justification that defies logic.

I suspect we should be more careful about what we're surrendering and for whom. I believe we need to work hard on our personal Echonomics so as to avoid the risks associated with imbalance – losing yourself for the sake of pleasing someone else who may not be worth it.

I think we should remember that even if someone or something seems like a worthy cause, the price of changing yourself might be higher than the potential benefit.

Ultimately, if we view our identity as the most important thing we have, we may react differently and more considerately to ourselves.

6. THE PRISM SAGA – a thought on the questions raised by the NSA/Prism situation

Only those who avoid the news will have missed the Edward Snowden 'whistle-blowing' saga involving a clandestine network called Prism.

This all kicked off as a result of a leaked powerpoint presentation, dated April 2013, that suggested US intelligence agencies had access to the servers of nine firms including Google, Microsoft, Facebook, Yahoo, Skype and Apple.

The Guardian then reported that the UK's electronic surveillance agency, GCHQ, had been able to see user communications data from American Internet companies because it had access to Prism.

I've waited for a while before writing this to let the reactions to the Prism saga settle and allow enough space to bring forward my perspective with the intention of de-cluttering the issue for others.

The way I see it is that the Prism saga is actually split into four defining questions:

1. Is Prism all that is going on?

Assuming that Prism exists as reported, do you think it is a fair or complete portrait of what is actually happening in the surveillance and security world? When commenting on the situation we may be tempted to speak in finite terms – in other words, classing the Prism saga as the entire situation.

Some could argue that we only see the leaked information that is allowed to be seen. Others could even argue that the Prism saga is designed for the bad guys to feel the heat, allowing a certain level of healthy paranoia amongst the innocent public. This point could follow the logic that those who are most guilty should be most concerned, but regardless the question still remains: do you think Prism is all that is going on?

2. Is surveillance necessary?

Here I'm referring to all types of 'snooping', 'spying' and 'monitoring' as surveillance. The judgement call one needs to make is whether a certain level of surveillance is necessary to ensure the security of our countries. There are many types of surveillance for different reasons, but in the context of the Prism saga this is allegedly surveillance of personal information.

Some could argue there is probably a line past which surveillance is an abuse of Civil Liberties but even if we assume there is a line in place, the question still remains: do you think surveillance is necessary?

3. Should the public know everything that is going on?

Many speak of total transparency but we should examine whether that would give us more or less comfort in the security of our countries. If you think we should have the basic human right to know, it is worth considering whether it would genuinely benefit our lives.

Some could argue that our level of happiness is partly due to knowing as much as we feel comfortable knowing. Even though some would claim that ignorance is sometimes bliss, the question still remains: should the public know everything that is going on?

4. Do you have faith or trust in the people who look after our security?

Many people think the Government runs the country. Others think it is rich business people or perhaps a Royal family or two. Depending on your version, this Latin phrase comes to mind: "Quis custodiet ipsos custodes?" (Who will guard the guards themselves?). Wherever you feel the control is, the level of faith or trust in that control is a major factor in forming a position on the Prism saga.

Some could argue that the surveillance itself isn't as much of an issue as how the information is used and by whom. It may be that the bigger picture is far more ugly or more positive, if we were to know who was pulling the strings. We could try and logically work it out, or prefer to believe in a certain version, but either way the question still remains: do you have faith or trust in the people who look after our security?

Evidently all four questions are linked together and you'd be right in feeling that it may (or may not) be a good idea to construct a version of events that you feel comfortable with and stick to your story.

7. A SECT CANNOT BE DESTROYED BY CANNONBALLS – a thought on the realities of dealing with de-centralised groups, from pirates to terrorists

Here are two quotes from the 1st/2nd May 2011:

"The world is a safer place, because of the death of Osama Bin Laden" President of the United States

"Is this the beginning of the end for the war on terror?" BBC News

…and one from 200 years ago:

"A sect cannot be destroyed by cannonballs" Napoleon Bonaparte

In nature and in business, the most common structure is for an organism or an organisation to be centralised. Spiders and a traditional bank are amongst the obvious examples. Centralised organisms and organisations feel the pain of attack on the main unit, for example, by the removal of food (in nature) or funding (in enterprise).

An alternative structure is one of decentralisation.

In these organisms and organisations, there is no main unit as the vital organs are distributed throughout the entire structure. Starfish are amongst the obvious examples in nature. Organisations such as Wikipedia, Craigslist and al Qaeda, are others.

Such decentralised structures handle attack in a totally different way from centralised ones. After all, if you chop off the head of a spider, it dies. Whereas if you chop off a leg of a starfish, it grows another leg – and the chopped leg grows into another starfish.

The news of the death of Osama Bin Laden, triggered me to refer to the work of Brafman and Beckstrom, authors of the vital transcript 'The Starfish and the Spider'[7]. In this book, they allude to moments in history that exemplify centralised versus decentralised structures. One example starts with the Aztecs.

In 1519 Hernando Cortes stared in disbelief at the Aztec metropolis Tenochtitlan. Expecting to see savages, instead he saw an organised and civilised community. Cortes witnessed a developed system of highways, ingeniously constructed aqueducts, spectacularly ornate temples, and mystically intriguing pyramids.

He also saw gold. Everywhere.

Cortes arranged a meeting with Montezuma II, the leader of the Aztecs. His conversation was not a friendly one – it was a monologue that could be summed up with "give me your gold, or I will destroy you".

Montezuma believed that Cortes might be a deity and decided to yield his vast resources. Shortly after that, Cortes repaid Montezuma's trust and submission by killing him, placing the city under siege, and cutting off its food and water supplies. Within 80 days 240,000 were dead – within 2 years, the civilisation had collapsed.

Less than a decade later Francisco Pizarro captured and killed the leader of the Incas, Atahuallpa. They, too, were plundered, and within two years the society became an historical footnote.

Over a century later the conquering Spanish headed to the deserts of modern day New Mexico to force a Christian conversion upon the natives there. They would make them Catholics – they would transform them from hunters into farmers.

The primitive people were the Apaches. The Apaches had nothing – except their way of life. No highway system. No permanent towns or cities. No pyramids. No gold. All that was valued was stored under their dark skin – in their immense souls.

For two centuries the Apache battled the Spanish tooth and nail. The wild people of the deserts persevered and prevailed. Why? Because every one of them fought from a spiritual compulsion, rather than the command-and-control coercion of officers and strategy.

The Apache had no appointed chief or army commander, but they did have the Nant'an.

A Nant'an was a spiritual leader who led by example – not by coercion. Warriors fearlessly followed the Nant'an. Nant'ans lived, fought, and died alongside those they led. When one was killed, another seemed to incarnate the spirit of the fallen and press the fight forward. Inspired. Courageous. They resisted. Not because they had to, but because they wanted to.

The Apache have no word or concept for the phrase – "you should".

Not one of those proud Native Americans had to follow their larger-than-life leaders. Neither Geronimo nor Cochise roared "you should", "you must" or "follow me".

Apaches were empowered to choose against whom, and if, they would make war.

When the Spanish killed a Nant'an, a new one would take his place. Like Agent Smith in The Matrix[8].

When they burned a village, the Apache became nomadic.

The more they were attacked, the more decentralised and resilient the Apache became.

The Apaches won because of their decentralised structure, based on deep relationships, in the absence of leadership, hierarchy and rules. This deep affinity with one another was the primary tool of this insurgency.

Then it all went wrong…

The Americans (of European descent) entered the picture. They too found it impossible to defeat the Apaches.

Until, that is, they decided to give them some land and a few cattle.

Within a few years the Apache society had fallen apart.

You may question why land and cattle would trigger such destruction of something so decentralised and resilient. And rightly so. In fact, I attest that these lessons are critical to humanity, not just in a political sense of rulership, but also at a sociological level of understanding. Especially in the context of recent events.

It turns out, there are three ways of destroying decentralised structures.

1. Change the participants' ideology by showing them another, better, way
2. Centralise them by giving them constructs in which greed is built
3. Decentralise yourself

This particular chapter is not intended for a full exploration of how the above three points can take shape – but evidently, the Apaches were destroyed by the second method.

In light of the Osama Bin Laden events, and without attempting some political advisory role, or religious bias, I would say this:

1. It would be wise to view the horrific, terrorist acts as manifestations of decentralised, asymmetric warfare
2. It would not be as wise to view this horror as removable, nor reconcilable, by the murder of one man

3. It would be wise to rapidly strategise, distribute, and execute a counteractive plan that takes into extreme context, the very nature of the structural elements involved in the challenge
4. It would not be as wise to celebrate a temporary passing as outright victory, with all respect to lives lost forthwith

As a pacifist and humanitarian, my personal belief is that the demise of others is not an acceptable way of promoting a singular cause. Thus, I give this free advice based on bias toward a more harmonious world, rather than one of conflict.

Nevertheless, if a country, Government or movement is setting out to truly combat acts of terror, the infrastructure of the challenge should be considered in the highest regard.

PART TWO: TECHNOLOGY

8. FROM KINETICS TO MEANING – a thought on finding the purpose behind modern technology

"Canst thou send lightnings, that they may go and say unto thee, Here we are?" Job 38:35

During the 19th century when electricity made its way into our lives there was much discussion about what electricity actually was. Commentators had no prior reference points with which to compare this new concept, however many had an opinion. One scientific writer named Dionysius Lardner summarised this at the time by stating: "The world of science is not agreed to the physical character of electricity."

Electricity was believed by a number of people to be fluid-like, lighter and more subtle than any gas; others suspected electricity was a compound of two fluids "having antagonistic properties"; whilst some thought it was more like sound "a series of undulations or vibrations". From the early telegraphs there were incredible announcements showing that electricity could make a gold leaf move, a pencil turn, or a curtain blow. The wonder and fascination was immense. The coolest people in the world were those who could tell you what else electricity could do.

Depending on your research into 19th century thinking on this subject, you may have your own favourite, but mine is a comment by Harpers Magazine in 1854 that read: "We are not to conceive of the electricity as carrying the message that we write, but rather as enabling the operator at the other end of the line to write a similar one."

I find this to be an interesting placement of the medium as being solely a supporting role to the main characters of sender and recipient, enabled to communicate. Harpers were perhaps suggesting that the fascination with what is carrying the message should be de-prioritised in favour of what it means for the two 'operators' to be in contact.

Throughout history the placement of our fascination is a determining factor for how industries, careers, and societies are formed. Sometimes, however, the most visible aspect is not the most important.

As an example, let us fast forward to the present day.

Just as electricity re-defined the lives and value chains before, the Internet, and the increasing capability and affordability of technology, is re-defining all that we know. We are at the early stages of this disruption, and even the most cynical are becoming aware that nothing is as it was.

At the time of writing, in July 2012, an increasingly popular topic is 'The Internet of Things'. This was a term first used in 1999 by Kevin Ashton, the British technology pioneer who co-founded the Auto-ID Centre at MIT, which created a global standard system for RFID and other sensors. His definition of 'The Internet of Things' was a system where the Internet is connected to the physical world via ubiquitous sensors. As it happens, prior to this work at MIT, he was a brand manager at P&G in 1997 where he got interested in how RFID could help manage P&G's supply chain.

Since then, and like a child with a new toy, our tendency is to be drawn into the new possibilities of fridges populating shopping lists, pepper mills telling waiters a refill is needed, or car engines alerting garages that a service is required. Yet I feel it is just as important that we take time to reflect and consider what all this super-connectivity actually means for society and life in general.

If our objects can remove tasks that make up much of our lives, what will we fill those holes with?

If the majority of our workforces carry out jobs that can be increasingly automated, what will those people do instead?

Is there a limit to what we seek to enable connection of?

Do we require limitations on the freethinking within connections?

There are so many questions I suspect we should ask – but primarily there is one over-riding point I believe we need to discuss further:

Can the information generated by pervasive connectivity be sufficiently filtered to avoid being drowned in unnecessary noise?

When stuff is connected to each other, noise is created. This noise can be data, transactions, or any information that is sent and received. Depending on your objective and function, this could be necessary or not. Unnecessary noise in this context is noise that is not needed by an object, task, or individual.

Of course, if your objective or function is around the subject of Big Data, the more data/noise the better. Apparently. In reality this seems to often eclipse the passion for more useful data and in terms of media, reach is considered to win over specificity and hard science tends to beat soft in a straight fight. Many seem attracted to noise over signal; in fact the noise becomes the signal.

Ultimately it is purpose that differentiates what each person's signal and noise is and I predict an eventual shift towards that realisation. A shift towards an answer to the question: How much extra noise will it take until our fascination is forced to be in the methods of filtering? Perhaps then we may see business models in lessening rather than gaining? Companies that set out to remove clutter and distraction, to focus on what really matters. Reduction rather than production. A tipping point in the level of nonsense in our lives…

Currently I see context-addition services that, for example, add a tagline to a photo, or link a shared experience with nearby friends. These are perfectly valid, but extending this further into other stuff that is super-connected we'll soon be able to share an experience with a static object like a fridge, and the fridge will be able to respond. When this happens we're not talking about a miniscule 5 billion connected mobile devices, we're talking hundreds of billions of things. Masses of stuff that is connected together.

You know what this sounds like? It sounds like the next media channel deemed to be exploitable. I foresee a 'Head of the Internet of Things'. Actually it's already here.

If mobile's USP is that it is a personal device at the control of an individual (a point sadly ignored amongst many practitioners), I wonder what the USP of connected things is? How do you try and apply a traditional advertising approach to a lampshade? Actually, that's already here too.

Maybe, in fact, we should take a step back and reflect.

Maybe we could create a situation where connected stuff exists predominantly so our lives become easier and more enjoyable to live. Again, a subjective point but I wonder if there isn't room for more of that bias towards societal betterment in our thinking?

Are we absolutely sure we're creating a utopian, rather than a dystopian, future for ourselves?

I guess we will find out in due course, probably being alerted by some form of sensor on a currently inanimate object.

9. VALUE CHAIN DISRUPTION IN 3D – a thought on how 3D printing and similar innovation may disrupt many parts of business

Over the last few years my standard answer to the question "What is the next big thing?" has been 3D printing.

Initially, reactions ranged from disbelief through to downright fear for my sanity.

I've called for us to change our mental image of what 'printing' is. It's currently a 2D concept. Ink goes onto paper, inked paper comes out.

With 3D, imagery goes in, product comes out.

In a Sunday Times Review, Matt Rudd wrote a piece called "Next, we'll print out a curly iPhone" and shared information about a company called RepRap who, in fact, are one of many in this space. My favourite part of the article was the quote: "a senior Google figure says we should think of RepRap as a China on your desk… If we all have factories in our own homes, what will happen to industry?"

Rudd touches briefly on the answers to this question, but I think the question deserves more. I'll say it right here, right now:

I believe 3D printing will disrupt the entire value chain of manufacture, distribution, purchase and consumption.

It's imperative to look past today's capabilities of the reasonably expensive and slow 3D kit, and think about what your mobile phone looked like 10 years ago.

I predict that by the end of this decade, if you smash a glass on the floor at a dinner party, you'll simply be able to print another one out.

If you want to try on a pair of trainers, print them out, try them on. Don't like them? Throw them in your energy recycler, which powers your house.

Think about the implications to healthcare. What does it mean if you can print out drugs? What does 3D printing mean to the prosthetic industry?

What about car parts? Will you need to go to a shop for car mats if you can just produce one with a single click?

Imagine what will happen when your desktop unit can print out circuit boards. Want a new phone every day – just select daily repeat.

But enough fanciful thought. The questions I ask you to consider are:

If you're a brand – where does this leave you?

If you're a logistics company – where does this leave you?

If you're a retail outlet – where does this leave you?

Where do you earn your money if I am now your factory and retailer?

If I can create my own wireless chip you normally provide when mine is faulty, how are you going to charge me when you don't do anything for it?

The IP questions here are rife. How is it legislated or regulated?

If I owned a company that sold physical products, I would be seriously considering where we fit in a world in which our factories, distribution systems and retail outlets are inside individual homes.

If those individuals don't respect and trust us, why would they share any of the upside with us?

My rhetoric elsewhere about creating armies of fanatics may not seem so rhetorical, when your survival in the market is directly proportional to the level of respect and trust by your individual manufacturers.

I'm glad the discussion looks slightly less 'crazy-talk' as it's been a struggle to convince people this is on the agenda.

Actually, it's not just on the agenda. It is the agenda.

"Ineluctable modality of the visible: at least that if no more…" James Joyce (Ulysses)

10. EMOTION IN ARTIFICIAL INTELLIGENCE – a thought on whether the progress of intelligent technology is necessarily beneficial to humans

In 1992, Gerald Tesauro created a programme called TD-Gammon at IBM's Thomas J. Watson Research Centre. The TD part stands for Temporal Difference (which is a type of learning system), and the Gammon part is taken from the game, Backgammon.

TD-Gammon quickly became as competent as the world's best human players, eventually beating them and showing unforeseen strategies that, to this day, are incorporated by humans in backgammon tournaments. The real innovation was actually within the evaluation process used by the programme. Basically, the algorithm became more and more consistent with every move, improving the view of the board and probabilities, based on the most recent move (hence temporal-difference learning). The capability to dynamically learn got the Artificial Intelligence (AI) community pretty excited.

A year later, in 1993, a guy called Vernor Vinge[9] a mathematics professor, computer scientist and science fiction writer, wrote a book called 'The Coming Technological Singularity: How to Survive in the Post-Human Era'[10].

This is how the book starts:

"Within thirty years, we will have the technological means to create superhuman intelligence. Shortly after, the human era will be ended.

Is such progress avoidable? If not to be avoided, can events be guided so that we may survive? These questions are investigated. Some possible answers (and some further dangers) are presented.

What is The Singularity?

The acceleration of technological progress has been the central feature of this century. I argue in this paper that we are on the edge of change comparable to the rise of human life on Earth. The precise cause of this change is the imminent creation by technology of entities with greater than human intelligence. There are several means by which science may achieve this breakthrough (and this is another reason for having confidence that the event will occur):

• The development of computers that are "awake" and superhumanly intelligent. (To date, most controversy in the area of AI relates to whether we can create human equivalence in a machine. But if the answer is "yes, we can", then there is little doubt that beings more intelligent can be constructed shortly thereafter)

• Large computer networks (and their associated users) may "wake up" as a superhumanly intelligent entity

• Computer/human interfaces may become so intimate that users may reasonably be considered superhumanly intelligent

• Biological science may find ways to improve upon the natural human intellect"

Vinge later writes that "I'll be surprised if this event occurs before 2005 or after 2030."

It may come as a surprise that Vinge wasn't the first writer who went to these apparent extremes.

In 1847, R. Thornton, the editor of the Primitive Expounder[11], wrote (more than half in jest) about the recent invention of a four function mechanical calculator:

"…such machines, by which the scholar may, by turning a crank, grind out the solution of a problem without the fatigue of mental application, would by its introduction into schools, do incalculable injury. But who knows that such machines when brought to greater perfection, may not think of a plan to remedy all their own defects and then grind out ideas beyond the ken of mortal mind!"

And also, a hero of mine Alan Turing[12] stated in 1951 that:

"Once the machine thinking method has started, it would not take long to outstrip our feeble powers … At some stage therefore we should have to expect the machines to take control."

More recently (and fashionably), in a 2005 book by Ray Kurzweil 'The Singularity Is Near'[13], the first chapter discusses what Kurzweil calls The Six Epochs. The penultimate epoch is called 'The Merger of Human Technology with Human Intelligence'.

This epoch, giving further emphasis to Vinge, is where technology reaches a level of sophistication and fine-structuring comparable with that of biology, allowing the two to merge to create higher forms of life and intelligence. Kurzweil claims that we are now in the process of entering this epoch, thus giving justification to his claims that The Singularity is near.

So far, so good.

The Singularity is a very popular topic now. Those who are really into proper geek technology, have a field day with imagining what life may look like when computers outstrip human capabilities.

There are detractors of course, however the challenges I find most interesting are lesser found in common reviews and posts about The Singularity or AI in general. The challenge I'm fascinated with is:

Can non-benevolent (i.e. non-well meaning) super-intelligence persist?

To this point there was poignant commentary in a piece in 2011 by Mark Waser[14]. Here's an excerpt:

"Artificial intelligence (AI) researchers generally define intelligence as the ability to achieve widely-varied goals under widely-varied circumstances. It should be obvious, if an intelligence has (or is given) a malevolent goal or goals, that every increase in its intelligence will only make it more capable of succeeding in that malevolence and equally obvious therefore that mere super-intelligence does not ensure benevolence."

My favourite quote from Mark is at the end of his post:

"A path of non-benevolence is likely to come back and haunt any entity who is not or does not wish to be forever alone in the universe."

And this brings me to a point of view still under development in my mind… and to be honest, I'm shocked there is such low volume of writing and apparent thought in this area.

I'm concerned that the people most involved with AI are primarily technologists. In the same way as Mark Zuckerberg defines privacy, identity, and human rights in a totally different way than I do, I'm concerned that the proponents of AI are considering a different definition of benevolence.

The intelligence spoken of is the type necessary to win at backgammon, or chess – activities that have ultimate scenarios and finite variables. The machine intelligence involved in developments of The Singularity and AI is contextually logical and mathematical. There is little talk of the illogical and emotional, because the machinery being developed, albeit of exponential capability, is fundamentally hierarchical, not democratic like the human brain. We seem to overlook there is a reason why even the smartest computers cannot beat the best players at poker.

I fear that the intelligence involved is only one part of the intelligence that powers humankind. I struggle to believe that the emotional intelligence has been featured strongly enough in AI computations.

Whilst my personal hope is for benevolent super-intelligence, I'm hard pressed to find enough proof that the AI developments are considering the soft science elements as an equal priority.

And let's not forget, the estimation of our own emotional intelligence is at best embryonic. It is only in recent times that we have started to realise the deep cognitive patterns that power our thoughts, decisions and behaviours.

Ultimately I'm concerned that we haven't even scratched the surface of our own emotional intelligence, so how prepared are we to ensure optimal artificial emotional intelligence, if indeed that is even a priority?

11. QUANTIFYING BIOCRIME – a thought on the future of biological crime

The Nike Fuelband is just one of many examples within a movement known as 'Quantified Self'. In simple terms this is basically a process of being aware of what we do and how it affects us. For instance, knowing that by running two miles you burn a certain number of calories, or that in a day you've walked a certain number of steps.

Moving forward we'll see more tools appearing that enable us to access the data we're producing and at the time of writing in the middle of 2013, the vast majority of comment is about the positive opportunities data recording brings. For Nike, last year's profits rose by 18% in their equipment division due to the launch of the Fuelband, and for the public, it would appear we like recording and observing a lot of what we're doing and, at times, sharing it with others.

This habit of recording, observing and sharing may seem fairly trivial when it only involves calories burned but we're on the brink of unlocking a new level in our personal information. The game is already in play and it involves the most advanced storage system in the universe that holds the most detailed personal information on each and every one of us.

Our DNA.

In terms of 'self' there is no purer version and the moves toward quantifying it are rapidly taking shape, a subject well covered in Wired Magazine in recent times, inspiring this piece in many ways.

Scientists have been onto this for ages too. The first human genome sequence cost £2billion to complete in the year 2000, today it's less than £2500 and by the end of the decade it will cost less than a pound. As you read this, genetic engineers are programming living things directly all over the world. To aid this effort, thousands of people have proactively shared their complete genetic codes and other biometrics to the Public Genome Project.

On the good side we can envisage new possibilities in 'life betterment' such as medicines and disease control, on the downside there's a high chance we are moving into an era of BioCrime.

If you view living organisms as computers, the hardware is the cell and the operating system software is our personal DNA. In short, what we currently know as computer hacking will likely be mirrored in DNA hacking.

After all, if genetic engineering becomes as common as software engineering, there will be millions of new developers in the field and it's extremely likely (if not inevitable) that sociopaths and terrorists will be involved.

If we look at the range of digital hacks and ask what the BioCrime versions would be, there are some pretty bleak outcomes that could well be round the corner. For now, I'll resist talking about mass genocide and vicious denial of service attacks of entire cities but instead focus in on four BioCrime scenarios that would appear to be waiting in the wings.

BioSpam

As with computer spam, it's all about volume. It isn't targeted very much; it's just a numbers game.

Bringing the methodology across to BioCrime you could envisage the creation of synthetic bacteria that can easily be distributed to a small group and realistically could spread like a common cold. This could blanket the world in months.

It so happens that pattern formation is already supported in synthetic creations so people could suddenly develop rashes on their skin with logos or other imagery on. Even by writing that I imagine the media industry dreaming up a new terminology. Rash Marketing or some such… Rash is the new Reach… oh boy.

Seriously though, one could imagine new industry verticals opening up with companies distributing anti-spam technologies from synthetic vaccines to body-covering equipment to avoid contact with the spreading BioSpam bacteria. If you are in an anti-virus company today, this may be your next market opportunity.

BioSpoofing

Taking DNA and placing it somewhere else could quite easily frame someone at the scene of a crime they were nowhere near.

In an article published by the Journal of Forensic Sciences International, researchers demonstrated it is possible to isolate DNA from a tissue or glass and mass-produce it. For instance a piece of skin could be grown or in-vitro sperm produced that frames someone for sexual assault.

Can you imagine the level of policing this would require and the advancement in biotechnology to counteract it? And what type of tools could individuals use to protect themselves from being 'BioSpoofed'?

BioPhishing

500 million times a day an official looking email requests a recipient to open links that then steal information.

In the digital world it is more possible to *not* leave a 'signature' but biologically we leave parts of us everywhere. Signatures with extraordinary volumes of data inside that are way more detailed than any digital interaction we carry out. We may be paranoid about technology companies seeing our passwords but that's nothing in comparison to what we're already leaving behind.

We're always shedding skin cells for a start. Then there's the saliva left on every cup or item of cutlery, and taxis and plane seats covered in our hair. Hotel bathrooms and beds provide an ideal location for BioPhishing with various fluids left around, all providing material to be used in the same way as our passwords are used when our email accounts are hacked.

Hairstylists and waiters may not seem so innocent in the future and your sewage system could easily be tapped for more private information than you've ever even told anyone. 'Knowing your shit' takes on a whole new meaning.

The DNA of unborn children doesn't even escape the threat as baby cells can be automatically sorted out of a mother's blood sample unwillingly left on a toothbrush.

One could imagine the types of organisations that may combat this. Maybe clothing companies or furniture manufacturers could innovate in areas that show what you're leaving behind in terms of DNA?

Spear BioPhishing

This is a more personalised version of mass BioPhishing.

Spear BioPhishing is a personalised biological attack where viruses, cells or other nanoparticles are engineered to become activated only when in contact with a particular organism or individual(s).

This could manifest like wiping the short-term memory of a particular group of people (like a shift of factory workers for example), or to ensure a particular politician loses his or her ability to speak…

Maybe the monitoring technologies could be used to monitor our relative sanity to check and alert us if any unusual activity is taking place? I'll resist the obvious punchlines here.

So while the Quantified Self movement is certainly full of funky ways to find out about our fitness and meaningful ways to find out about our core health:

1. We must move forward with awareness that the other side of the coin will be growing just as fast if not quicker. Don't only seek out the information that supports your preference or what suits your particular job, company or industry.

2. We must only build the future we want to live with. Everything you do has an impact on what is next. Question everything you are building today and check you're morally okay with the consequences of how things may play out if extended from today's version.

3. If you're a company looking for the next white space of

opportunity, the area of BioCrime is one you may not want to miss out on. In a positive way I hope. Start from considering the above four scenarios in terms of what the human need would be and how you could add extreme value.

PART THREE: PRIVACY

12. THE PRIVACY DILEMMA – a thought on who owns our data and the access to private information

We are living in a world where our trust can only come from respect of citizen privacy (preceded with credibility, authenticity, consistency and positive interactions).

Like many others, Facebook exists in an ongoing dilemma, which is something I get asked about often.

What it boils down to is this:

What if the most private information is the most valuable?

Do you:

A: Find even more subtle ways of getting it whilst keeping an increasingly suspicious public at bay?

Or:

B: Put citizens' privacy under their own control in an honest and decent way?

If the answer is B, then people's private information can only be gathered with their permission, which is therefore mandatory for understanding preference (which enables us to commercially communicate more effectively).

Elsewhere, a variety of tools enable you to run a diagnostic scan of your Facebook information to see what is secure and what is open to the public.

For some, the process is fairly simple and locking everything down to just 'friends' is do-able, however: do you absolutely trust everyone you ever added on Facebook to be so scrupulous with your information? Do you know for sure that they won't post a party picture elsewhere on the net?

We are simply scratching the surface of the Privacy Dilemma and as I have said many times, this is one of the main differentiators between the winning tools, platforms and channels in the future and the resources that get turned off en masse.

The multi-billion dollar valuation of Facebook looks seemingly indestructible but actually, their handling of the Privacy Dilemma leaves them, in my opinion, in a very fragile state.

There once was a site called 'Your Open Book' where one could scan all the public information that had been leaked by Facebook via a search engine. In this search engine you could enter anything from 'my boss' to 'rectal exam'. All the results were actual, real information that was publicly available, until it got removed from the web.

Around that time there was a 'Quit Facebook Day' on May 31st 2010 but only 12,877 committed to quit.

Why such a low number? I think it's a combination of:

1. A lack of awareness amongst people about how their information is being used
2. A lack of awareness of groups like the one featured above
3. A lack of understanding about what could happen if your personal information is out in the open
4. A lack of caring about the above

None of this moves me away from my view of how important this is and yes, I'm sure it's in the early stages of public awareness. I predict it will grow to be on the main agenda.

I'm not pushing for the closure of Facebook but whilst I have breath in my body I will campaign for the right of citizens to be in control of their own private information. I believe it is a basic human right and is central to our identity.

If you are thinking of innovating in the social network space, my free advice to you would be to differentiate around the issue of privacy. If you can still make the business model work, you will ultimately be better placed than the giants of today. For instance, businesses like Trsst[15], a private version of Twitter, could well be more relevant to our time than Twitter itself, ultimately.

The wider issue is how to change the behaviour of the other parts of a value chain, eagerly looking (and paying for) more and more personal information.

Ultimately, the dollars go where the people go; therefore it's down to every single one of us to stand up for ourselves and change the industry from the outside.

13. THE RISE OF SOCIAL NETWORK CLASS ACTION – a thought on the emergence of mass class action against social networks

In law, a class action or a representative action is a form of lawsuit in which a large group of people collectively brings a claim to court and/or in which a class of defendants is being sued.

This form of collective lawsuit originated in the United States and is largely heard of there. However, in several European countries with civil law (different from the English common law principle which is used by U.S. courts by the way), changes have been made in recent years that allow citizen (or consumer) organisations to bring claims on behalf of large groups of citizens (or consumers).

In recent times, class action lawyers have been quite busy with a new set of targets: social networking platforms. Facebook and Twitter are two that have recent filings against them.

In the lawsuit against Facebook, the lawyers are claiming, on behalf of numerous users under the age of 18 in New York, that Facebook does not receive parents' "permission before displaying that minors 'like' the products of its advertisers."

In the lawsuit against Twitter, the plaintiffs claimed that Twitter sent them an "unsolicited, confirmatory text message to their cellular telephone after they had indicated to Twitter that they no longer wanted to receive text message notifications." According to the lawsuit, the plaintiffs claimed that this act was in violation of the Telephone Consumer Protection Act. Spam, basically.

To a cynic, these actions may look like litigation-junkie opportunism. To others, like me, these actions (whilst potentially opportunistic) are just the tip of an iceberg that I predict will be increasingly revealed as we move forward – and I believe that the scale of class actions will rise, whilst the subject matter will continue to centre on data, identity and privacy.

I've publicly outlined the challenges that commerce has in terms of data, identity and privacy. In the previous chapter I asked a fundamental question:

What if the most private information is the most valuable?

Do you:

A: Find even more subtle ways of getting it whilst keeping an increasingly suspicious public at bay?

Or:

B: Put citizens' privacy under their own control in an honest and decent way?

I've also stated that whilst I'm not pushing for the closure of Facebook, I believe citizens should be in control of their own private information. I believe it is a basic human right and is central to our identity.

Now, whilst I didn't indicate the methods of citizens standing up for themselves, one could argue that these class actions are a method of doing just that.

If people enter into environments where their data is held and used, then at the very least, that information should be upfront, enabling people to have the freedom of choice. Not hidden within a cluster of terms and conditions or un-readable screens.

In my opinion, if companies run practices that are ethically questionable around the areas I've spoken about, I think the least they can expect is the odd class action now and again.

Actually, that's too subtle.

I predict we will see the demise of one or more social network platforms in the future, from mass class action, around unarguable and demonstrable evidence of malpractice in the context of human rights.

The reason I started this chapter with evidence is because the trend has already commenced.

Welcome to the rise of social network class action.

PART FOUR: DATA

14. THE BIG DATA DISASTER – a thought on the opportunities and risks of big data

If you are eager to understand and exploit the magnificent promise of big data, this post is for you. Alternatively, if you haven't really thought about big data yet, this is an early warning system. If you think that big data is the biggest news on the block and that the leading journalists, consultants and analysts can't possibly be wrong, here's an alternative viewpoint, for the record.

Summary Of Predictions

I've written a number of previous blog posts about big data, individual identity and resulting business decisions, however I suspect these have been too abstract, too early, or simply too long-winded! From many conversations with CEOs down, across multiple industries and from reading countless articles and publications relating to this hot topic, I feel it's time to briefly summarise my thoughts and although I can't compete with the louder voices selling in the dream of big data being the opportunity (I'm naming no names, nor linking to any external content), I'd like this chance to make things as clear as possible. Here goes:

Big Data Prediction 1: The financial forecasts for the promise of big data will be wide off the mark, causing a tidal wave of shock amongst companies that are neck deep in the totally unrealistic advice they've bought into

Big Data Prediction 2: Major expenditure will continue to happen despite targets not being hit; directors will be ousted, profit warnings will be common and eventually even the largest of company fortunes will plummet

Big Data Prediction 3: The very same people who extolled the virtues of big data will be retrospective experts in what went wrong and try desperately to come up with a new insight that covers over the cracks of what I'd generously term as malpractice

Big Data Prediction 4: Acquisitions made on the back of the big data promise will eventually be questioned for financial wrongdoing. Values will be written down and scandal will repeatedly hit the headlines, with analysts and commentators blaming accounting errors

Big Data Prediction 5: Then, the next hype cycle item will capture the imagination and boom, as we went from thinking it was all about digital to all about mobile, we'll go from all about big data to all about whatever is next

Alternatively, every organisation has an option to stop this nonsense right now and take a long hard look at the multiple layers of fiction that numerous organisations are buying as fact. Unfortunately too many are so far down the path it will only take a disaster to awaken the alternative. Organisations can either choose to change or have to change – most don't choose to and when they have to, they can't. There is across-the-board misjudgement of basic realities that are primarily considered either a) not as important as selfish financial gain or b) not as realistic as common understanding of how business works.

To answer these in order:

a) Selfish financial gain isn't going to win out in public anymore. Yes, maybe it worked before (nice yacht by the way) but now the public is super-empowered and connected by weapons of mass communication. Underestimate this at your peril.

b) The business world is progressing through a paradigm shift where everything down to an organisation's position in the value chain has been adjusted. No, I'm not saying what one knows about business is wrong – I'm saying the stuff one doesn't know about modern business is larger and more critical than one probably realises.

Whether you agree with my thesis or not, please keep my predictions in mind as you read through the papers. Look at the pages of the business news today (whatever day it is you read this). Which company is showing one of the five predictions to be true?

I bet you there is one.

Which prediction have I mentioned that is spookily manifesting, like a David Blaine trick, onto the newspaper in your hand or on your device? Look at it now and see.

Abracadabra. Magic isn't it?

Except it's not really. It's a sickening reality of how deep into the mess we've fallen.

Summary Of Reasoning

It is commonly thought by instigators of research in big data that most companies seek to use big data to understand customers/consumers better, and most have misunderstood the stark difference between personal data and non-personal data. Data that is generated from activities and events taking place is different from personal information that we may willingly or unwittingly share.

Either way, the basic fact is that the most accurate personal data is the most valuable, and (here's the key) that data happens to be the most private.

The fact that some companies think they can access or aggregate this now (without public concern), is no more valid than thinking you won't have a car crash in the future as you haven't had one in the past.

When I've talked about building trust through authenticity, I wasn't giving advice about marketing campaigns; I was talking about bullet-proofing your entire profit and loss.

When I suggested that soft science is now as important as hard numbers, I wasn't being some kind of afro-hippy; I was trying to save your company from alienating itself due to irrelevance.

This isn't trivial. This isn't something to think about next year. This is a decision you need to make right now.

Which side are you on? You choose…

A: You follow the hype bubble of big data and think that it's going to make you/your company rich – divorcing your human head from your corporate head as much as you can.

OR

B: You seriously consider the above words and ask yourself, as a human, are you in the game of exploiting information regardless of morality, or instead do you wish to pursue a purpose that people can believe in, and by doing so enable relationships of mutual value that will bring you profits beyond your imagination?

Yes, this is a binary choice. Right now.

Your move.

15. TRUE HARMONY IN DATA – a thought on the progression from flat to rich data

Believe it or not, the elementary understanding of the Greek Lyre, one of the first tuned musical instruments, is essential in understanding Greek Philosophy.

The basis of many mathematical and scientific findings, thus creating much philosophical discussion, originated from Pythagoras's experiments with string lengths and bridge positions on the seven- or eight-string Lyre.

Musical notes, and their relation to each other, are ratios.

An octave, generated by doubling a length of string, is 2:1. Shorten by a third and you get a fifth, expressed as 3:2.

The 'Harmonic Mean' redefined the general understanding of opposites, to see benefit in a blend of contradicting elements.

Things started to get (intentionally and experimentally) mixed up.

Blended.

This discovery of blending, be it high and low notes or wine and water, seemed at the time to be the world's greatest secret.

At this point Pythagoreans thought the body was strung like an instrument to a certain pitch. Health is to be 'in tune' but can be unbalanced if there is too much relaxation or tension of our human string.

The 'tonics' you buy as remedies from chemists are named from this origin.

Of course, things were not always this complex.

In fact, between the times of Pythagoras and Plato (depending on the material you read), there appeared to be a simple doctrine of a 'tripartite soul'.

Sounds complicated but it really isn't.

Basically it was said that people could be of three types:

1. Lovers of gain
2. Lovers of honour
3. Lovers of wisdom

Much categorisation followed this thinking, including the typecasting of guests at the Olympic Games:

1. Those who came to buy and sell (these were seen as the lowest class)
2. Those who came to compete (these were the next above the lowest)
3. Those who came to observe (these were the best class of all)

This simplicity is somewhat appealing but actually, despite the progression of thinking around established subjects, I find that many modern topics follow a similar, basic, compartmentalisation.

One modern and lesser-established area that generates typecasts is data mining, social analytics, social media monitoring and/or any other fancy term for what is basically:

A. Taking bucket loads of data and trying to make sense of it

Or, if you like:

B. The practice of taking what people post, say, publish or share and displaying it for money

In a similar way to our tripartite soul we have:

1. Those who exploit whatever is possible in terms of data, regardless of consequence
2. Those who bring solutions to market whilst trying to be respectful of the delicacies of using private data
3. Those who wish to watch, listen, learn, and think about the wider meaning of data exploitation

In a commercial world the ability to reside in type 3 is eclipsed by the requirement to pay a rent or mortgage, so realistically we can aspire to be in the 2nd camp, and in this particular chapter I won't be discussing those of the 1st type.

My point is, without a good measure of the 3rd, we often forego the ability to be respectful of the delicacies when using private data for commercial benefit.

In other words, we may try to commercialise in an honourable way, but whilst we do so we are unable to think seriously about the actual meaning of what we do. Due to this our attempts at being respectful are limited by how busy we are, the CEO's target, or shareholder expectation.

Often the version of respectfulness leaves a lot to be desired… and even then, quis custodiet ipsos custodes? Who verifies that our version of being reasonable is reasonable?

I see numerous tweets from funky-named companies in the field of social data but I wonder about the people (consumer, customers, users, the public) whose information is ultimately paying for the free bar at the VIP reception.

I see fabulously constructed websites but I wonder about the link between volume of data and what the hell it actually means.

I see brilliantly formed visualisations but I find it hard to reconcile these with actual business strategy. I mean real business strategy not "Facebook page strategy" or "mobile strategy".

There is seldom any link; other than a retrospective justification of required insight in some vain attempt to validate an already named tactic in search of a strategic objective.

There is seldom an efficient implementation; instead many companies are expecting some form of miracle result.

The thing is – you can find out who is speaking about you.

You can find out whether one platform is more used than another.

You can even find out who makes others click on something. Add this to the amount of followers they have (with some other cool stuff) and it turns out you have some form of new media credibility.

Allegedly.

But without a proper business strategy and an understanding of the psychological ramifications of data exploitation, what you are left with is a bunch of information that may or may not actually mean something.

You will be shown things with data that will blow your mind. You will be reading that data is the future… and you will be correct in exploring this path.

But.

I appeal to you to include some type 3. Include more thinking, assign more reflection time, find more reason, and take more learning.

I appeal to you to consider what it really means, over and above what it means to your business.

I appeal to you to determine the non-monetary cost of data to the people who are providing it.

And yes, returning to the analogy, eventually we may face the music. Just as music extrapolated the simplicity into blends, we may come across deeper meaning in all of this simplistic opportunism. We may look back at the present day and realise we only had a basic understanding of what was really going on.

Perhaps only then will we discover the subtleties and complexities that we currently discuss and exploit without significant due care. Perhaps only then will we start to create things that make a positive difference.

Perhaps only then will we find the true harmony in data.

PART FIVE: SAFETY

16. AN ONLINE SAFETY NOTE TO PARENTS – a thought on how to protect your children online

Would you feel uncomfortable knowing that your child was walking down a number of dark alleys at night to talk with complete strangers?

Would you be concerned if your child was giving away private information freely on street corners about your family home and personal circumstances?

Most parents, like myself, would naturally say yes.

Unfortunately, many children are involved in an online version of this activity whilst on the Internet without properly understanding the consequences. In part, this is because parents do not understand the consequences sufficiently and that is the reason this chapter was written.

The Reality

Increasingly there are more opportunities for children to get online – at home, at school and through their mobile phones and games consoles. This provides some great opportunities in terms of learning and communicating. However, the naive usage of social networking tools and platforms by children provides a feeding ground for a variety of sick individuals who you would normally do anything to protect your child from. The situations you would be fearful of are very similar online as they are offline. Security on the web, and across every social networking tool and platform, is an absolute priority in exactly the same way as locking the door to your house. The fact that your child may not have come to any harm to date, does not offer any guarantee they are not in danger right now, without even suspecting it.

Whilst it isn't productive to be paranoid, it is essential to understand what danger is out there. Whilst there are various police units dedicated to online safety and working hard at catching criminals, it's up to parents to provide the first line of defence.

According to the NSPCC[16] the Internet and related services present five main risks to children, namely:

- seeing disturbing information or images
- being the victim of online bullying (also known as cyberbullying)
- being contacted and manipulated by an adult for sexual purposes (also known as grooming)
- sharing personal and identifying information with strangers
- sending or receiving sexually explicit films, images or messages of themselves or others (this is known as sexting when sent by mobile phone)

You may have heard of these risks before, but you may not be aware of the scale of the issue:

- In a survey of 25,000 children by EU Kids Online[17] 14% of 9-16 year olds admitted they had seen sexual images on websites. This included 8% of 11-16 year olds who saw images of people having sex and/or genitals, and 2% who saw violent sexual images
- 32% of all 9-16 year olds who had seen sexual images said they were upset by them
- Among 11-16 year olds upset by seeing online sexual images, 26% hoped the problem would just go away, 22% tried to fix it, 19% deleted unwelcome messages and 15% blocked the

sender. Only 13% reported the problem online and most of those who did, found the result helpful

- 21% of 11-16 year olds have seen potentially harmful user-generated content such as hate sites (12%), pro-anorexia sites (10%, rising to 19% of 14-16 year old girls) and self-harm sites (7%). Those with greater digital skills are more likely to encounter these content-related risks
- According to a report by InternetSafety101[18], one in seven children has received a sexual solicitation online at some stage
- Over half (56%) of children sexually solicited online were asked to send a picture; 27% of the pictures were sexually-oriented in nature
- The majority of victims of Internet-initiated sex crimes were between 13 to 15 years old; 75% were girls and 25% were boys
- 9% of children in years 7 to 9 have accepted an online invitation to meet someone in-person and 10% have asked someone online to meet them in-person
- One in three parents (33%) claims to filter their child's Internet use and one in four (27%) uses monitoring software
- Overall, only a quarter of children (27%) and a third of parents think they are effective in helping to keep children safe online

Unfortunately, it isn't only parents who are unaware.

The lack of understanding by figures of authority or support in Government, schools, charities and even child protection services is concerning. For example, an online survey of 327 social workers[19] found 74% wanted more support, while half felt concerned about dealing with online sexual abuse or behaviour.

The survey also found that:

- 17% did not know how to "assess the risks" to a child when there was an "online dimension" such as Internet grooming
- 20% said they did not know the "warning signs" of what online sexual abuse looks like
- 43% lacked confidence about the language used by young people talking about the Internet, and more than a third said they did not know the right questions to ask in order to identify and assess online abuse

Looking deeper

Of the five main risks the NSPCC has outlined (and as mentioned previously), the two most commonly understood are:

- seeing disturbing information or images
- sharing personal and identifying information with strangers

The ways of reducing the risk of these are actually part of the same set of action points, outlined later in this chapter, addressing the other three risks:

- sending or receiving sexually explicit films, images or messages of themselves or others
- being the victim of online bullying
- being contacted and manipulated by an adult for sexual purposes

These are often the least understood and are all variations of abuse. It has been estimated that 1 in 4 children suffer some form of Internet harassment. Online bullying (cyberbullying) is an epidemic that is not necessarily carried out by bigger and stronger children. Even the quietest and mildest child has the most powerful weapon at their disposal which is humiliation and public ridicule through anonymous comments, threatening emails, modified or obscene photographs and text messages that spread rumours and gossip. Naturally the types of bully vary, yet the perpetrators are all armed with weapons of mass communication. It is perhaps easier to comprehend this relatively new type of bullying as so many of us have witnessed or experienced the original type ourselves.

However, 'grooming' is a lesser-known phenomenon, involving predators who attempt to build trust with your child in order to abuse them. Grooming usually starts with building a friendship and can take days or weeks to develop. Sometimes they arrange a set time to talk or meet with your child, reminding them not to tell you about it. Even when a child feels they should say something, they may feel that things have gone too far and they may be in trouble if they opened up to you. Here's some further reading on this from the NSPCC: http://www.nspcc.org.uk/news-and-views/our-news/nspcc-news/12-11-12-grooming-report/caught-in-a-trap-pdf_wdf92793.pdf

The polite 12-year-old girl your child has just met in a chatroom, who can't stop talking about her family's new pet and has just suggested meeting up for a smoothie, might well be a 53-year-old man with a much darker agenda. It is extremely easy for anyone to create a profile with false credentials that looks completely innocent. Predators intentionally don't look like predators, so despite trying to warn children away from interacting with suspicious profiles, it is those that look the most innocuous that often contain the biggest danger.

It is important to remember that for each image of child abuse, a child has been coerced, assaulted and badly hurt. Many will have been raped and, in a few tragic cases, the victim may even have been killed. That's the reality of modern paedophilia.

Recently the UK Government has promoted an initiative to make online pornography 'opt-in' – meaning that a household would need to unlock adult content. Unfortunately the leading official, Claire Perry MP, has confused pornography with child abuse, resulting in the theory that blocking online pornography will somehow restrict the sharing of child abuse material.

In reality, much of the sharing happens away from the version of the Internet you know it to be. A lot of the material is exchanged in what is known as the 'dark web', 'dark Internet' or 'deep web'. Unless you know how to get there, you won't find it; however it has been approximated by some to be significantly bigger than the worldwide web.

The dark web isn't searchable using Google and is totally anonymous. The dark web contains the majority of imagery that both Mark Bridger and Stuart Hazell viewed prior to the murders of 5-year-old April Jones and 12-year-old Tia Sharp. Here's some further reading in The Mirror: http://www.mirror.co.uk/news/uk-news/deep-web-drugs-guns-assassins-1337131

Last year the Child Exploitation and Online Protection (CEOP) Centre estimated that there were between 50,000 to 60,000 individual offenders identified as sharing abusive images of children. The study found a 70% year-on-year rise in the number of images with girls under 10 and a 125% rise in the number of online images featuring sex with children. Here's some further reading on this from ITV: http://www.itv.com/news/update/2013-05-28/ex-ceop-chief-child-abuse-figures-deeply-concerning/

One offender, Andrew Lintern, a married 55-year-old IT professional, was found with 20,000 indecent images, including video-clips of a 17-month-old baby being assaulted.

Interestingly, the leading adviser to the Government for online safety, John Carr, said "determined paedophiles…while they are very dangerous, they are a small number." It is up to each parent to decide whether 50,000 to 60,000 is a comfortably low number of UK individuals sharing what are, essentially, images of crime scenes involving thousands of abused children.

Advice for parents

Study this information carefully. Search deeper into the topic and become as well versed as you possibly can. Explain the risks in a way that you know will deeply resonate with your child.

- Make an agreement with your child as to the amount of time they can be online, what is acceptable to share with others and what level of interaction is acceptable with strangers.

- Learn how every device works and join every social network that your child uses. It may be complicated so find someone who can show you – maybe your child is best placed to do so.

- Ensure your child knows how to take screenshots and copy/paste content. It is really important they feel that there are no restrictions in telling you about their experiences and showing you evidence.

- Set up parental controls on every single device with Internet access including phones, tablets and even entertainment systems such as a PlayStation, Xbox, etc.

- Set up an account on every single portable device (e.g. phones, tablets, etc.) that enables you to locate where the device is at any time. These services (like http://www.lookout.com for example) often contain other security software that scans websites and applications to ensure safety.
- Do regular web searches (and image searches) for your child's real names, any known screen names, email addresses and phone numbers.

- Look deeper into the different language your child may be using. For example, you may have a filter for the term 'porn' but not 'pron' that is often more common. Another example is 'warez' which is illegally obtained software. 'Paw' stands for 'parents are watching' and 'pos' means 'parents over shoulder'.

- Encourage the use of devices in family areas rather than in bedrooms or other enclosed spaces.

- Notice changes of behaviour. Is your child getting online at a similar time every day? Are they secretive when using devices, for example, turning the screen off suddenly or refusing to tell you what they've been doing? Does their mood change immediately after using devices? Are they very happy or very sad? These are all signs that they may be forming new relationships that fall outside of what you would allow.

- Store these details and use the sites as a source of reference (and I apologise for the UK centricity of these links): Get Safe Online (for advice on most matters regarding how to stay safe) https://www.getsafeonline.org/ - Stop it Now 0808 1000 900,

Website: http://www.stopitnow.org.uk - NSPCC Helpline 0808 800 5000, Website: http://www.nspcc.org.uk - Childline 0800 1111, Website: http://www.childline.org.uk

- If something untoward does happen, a useful process to remember for you and your child is:

    - STOP (stop interacting with the person immediately)

    - RECORD (take screenshots, keep dates, times, and texts, emails or other content)

    - BLOCK (most services have a form of blocking or limiting contact)

    - REPORT (either to you, the school if applicable or helpline/authorities number)

Although these pieces of advice may seem longwinded and involve some effort to develop, it is undeniable that the risks involved with online activity are increasing and we all have a duty of care in ensuring the safety of our children by understanding the dangers to a satisfactory level and taking preventative action.

PART SIX: ADVOCACY

17. ADVOCURRENCY – a thought about an alternative trading currency for the advertising industry

I remember reading in Smash Hits magazine when I was young about how Keith Richards from The Rolling Stones would drape coloured scarves over lampshades to get the right ambience backstage.

Spin forward a few years and I found myself backstage at my own gig, setting off the fire alarm by a scarf catching fire against a bare lightbulb. It turned out the lampshade part was critical when impersonating 'Keef' due to it shielding the bulb. Mind you, that's the nearest I got.

Placing a scarf over a lampshade is a way of changing the output of a product. It's a remix, an edit – a mashup. It need not be authorised.

The lack of authorisation isn't a problem unless you start a fire, however the makers of the lamp and lightbulb most likely didn't intend, nor predict, their design would be edited. The lamp, and any appended shade, is intended to be the de facto creation. The creators spend time making it just right, sometimes they hire people to invent an accompanying story so people are engaged, the venue owners place it in just the right place, and the electricity suppliers ensure the power turns it on.

Our role as benefactors of the light is to be enlightened.

And that alone.

Now let's use this analogy and apply it to the advertising world.

Imagine the creators of the lamps are all of the brand owner companies and the advertising agencies are the ones who create the accompanying lamp stories – making the lamps look and feel fabulous and attractive.

Imagine the media agencies as the ones who plan where the lamp should be in the room.

Obviously it is the public who are the electricity suppliers – powering the above.

However, the public is also able to throw scarves over the lamps, amending what the lamp looks and feels like… This is a secondary role that is fairly modern, has massive consequences, and is primarily due to the huge disruption that the Internet brought to the commercial communication landscape.

Here's how:

Whereas media channels like TV are currently used for one-way broadcast, the newer channels (enabled by the Internet) have a feedback mechanism, providing the ability to interact and converse.

Actually the affordability and capability of technology has risen so significantly that many people (but not all) now have the ability – that used to reside only in the corporate domain – to create, edit, and publish information. If you like, the everyday citizen is armed with weapons of mass communication.

This world of exchangeable opinion has led to brands being democratised. Brands can be remixed, edited, and mashed up, without any authorisation from the companies that own the branded product or service, nor the representative agency.

The general public is empowered with not only the scarves to throw over the lamps, but also the technology to share their new scarf/lamp creation with the world.

To these 'brand remixers' it is now their brand. The opinion of theoretical brand owners is largely irrelevant, and if stated, is largely rejected. This is because the publicly perceived attitude and behaviour of an official brand is often one of hierarchical patronisation, which worked well in the one-way world yet plays out sub-optimally in our modern, multi-way interactive environment.

The reality and scale of brand democratisation is such that I'm often asked what the potential ways of doing business are, where the revenue will come from, and how an agency needs to operate if they are to maximise the opportunity.

Advertising agencies are appointed by companies (a.k.a clients) to create brands and metaphors that (hopefully) will resonate with prospective customers, who (hopefully) buy, and love, the product or service. Clients could do it themselves, theoretically, but most appoint an agency.

Advertising agencies are commonly paid by companies per job, on a retainer, or a mixture of the two. Agencies are mostly reactive to what a company has decided it needs (even if the agency thinks it is coming up with everything itself), and are often forced to do more work for less money as budgets are cut and/or procurement drives prices down.

Not to put too fine a point on it, when a client says jump it's not uncommon for agencies to ask "how high and for how long?" After all, an agency is funded by its clients. Exclusively.

Rather than being paid for the value created, agencies tend to be paid for their time. Proposals are mostly constructed from an equation of how many people would be needed and for how much time. Often an agency will use existing staff and take percentages of people's time into account, for instance; 25% of Sally, 50% of Tim, and 15% of Jill. Often Sally, Tim, and Jill will be included in other things also and it is fairly normal to have over 100% of time accounted for. You can imagine where that leaves everyone.

When examining future revenue models for advertising agencies it is imperative to start from a position of clarity about existing revenue models, cost bases, and client relationships. In most cases, when dealing with an agency of pedigree, the task for constructing new ways of working isn't solely down to dreaming up other ways of doing business, but instead defining a vision, establishing a purpose, applying the existing context, then plotting a way forward between today's situation, and tomorrow's aspiration.

Within all this, the control is not within the agency – it is within the client. Thus it would be prudent to assume the future revenue models and ways of working need to be agreeable to clients and the business environment in which they trade – assuming little change in the reactive versus proactive nature of the relationship in the short/medium term.

I say this because, to my mind, advertising agencies are trading as if they are in the business of production. Reactive production rather than proactive production.

Reactive production is all about churning out adequate stuff at the cheapest price whilst retaining a margin that allows trade to continue. It is about using the resources at hand to best address instruction from on high, in the most efficient manner possible. This isn't to say the expertise isn't there but put bluntly, it's a numbers game.

In my opinion, advertising agencies should actually be in the business of representative facilitation.

It's a bit of a mouthful, but representative facilitation is the practice of making it possible for those who (in word or deed) stand up for a product or service in the marketplace – to better do so.

I think advertising agencies should be in the game of ensuring people have a wide choice of scarves to put over lamps, and to enable the sharing of creations with others.

I think advertising agencies can do their job (of making lamps look and feel fabulous) better, if they took into account the interpretations of remixers and editors who are not on the payroll. A scarf-covered lamp is a clear indication of adjusted preference.

In the commercial communication world there could be firms that may feel they are sort of in this area already. Public Relations (PR) agencies could imagine they sit here, as could Word Of Mouth (WOM), Social Media (SM) and even Direct Marketing (DM) agencies who often take care of the Customer Relationship Management (CRM) for a client.

But none of them actually are.

All of them are involved in representation but seldom in the true facilitation of representation. This isn't a criticism – just a difference in interpretation.

The PR agencies will monitor the scarf usage and ensure the key messages are repeated with the hope that users remember how important the underlying lamp is.

The WOM and SM agencies will engage in discussion about the usage of scarves to cover lamps, but ideally want some positive sentiment about the lamp itself – even if the discussion shows the scarf is actually the main thing and the lamp is a by-product.

The DM and CRM agencies will continually target the lamp owners with very little knowledge of whether scarves were ever used. The prime objective is to sell more lamps rather than build relationships regardless.

I should state I have no bias towards advertising agencies getting more involved in the facilitation of scarf throwing and sharing – the opportunity is there for any player type, it just seems that the original creative work is the amended subject in this case, thus one would think the creatives have an option for further involvement.

If my suggested approach were to be considered, the revenue stream options would fall mostly into that of reputation and relationship management. These are loyalty-based mechanisms like:

- transactional commission on returning custom driven by loyalty
- platform license fees for sharing tools that enable the spread of opinion
- share of saved expenditure (acquisition/marketing/PR etc) due to ongoing positive sentiment

I call all of this 'Advocurrency'.

This is a multi-dimensional currency that exchanges advocacy for a tradable currency, usable for buying, redeeming, and relating. Advocurrency exists already, but it's currently only used in one dimension (at the time of writing).

For instance, Uniqlo ran a campaign where the sale price of certain items was reduced each time someone on twitter mentioned #luckycounter.

That's a really basic version of one dimensional advocurrency.

The Palms Hotel in Las Vegas and the Four Seasons in New York both treat guests differently if they have a significant online influence. One gives free iPads for the duration of the stay, the other gives you an entirely separate VIP check in.

Again, one dimension.

The next dimension for advocurrency will be how industry uses it to trade.

Holistically, my view is captured by Edith Wharton, the American novelist who died in 1937: "There are two ways of spreading light: to be the candle or the mirror that reflects it."[20] I think agencies should be in the mirror industry now.

I believe we could create 'sentixchanges' which convert positive sentiment, harnessed by an agency, into real world monetary value over and above the resultant trade.

I believe we could create trading agreements where the loyalty and opinion of armies of fanatics is paid for in a similar way to market research, with a share going to every party involved on the trade and consumer side.

Here's an example – just for starters:

Agency Y co-creates campaigns with members of Brand Z's fan club. The new campaign brings more people into the fan club and the widened positive sentiment has a recognisable impact on the level of repeat engagement with Brand Z's service.

The repeat engagement shows increased purchase volumes by a certain % and Agency Y takes a commission on each purchase value, thus realising £X.

This repeat engagement also has an Advocurrency value of (e.g.) 300 that converts into £X of billing between Brand Z and Agency Y.

The Advocurrency value of 300 can be passed to members of the fan club by way of payment, rewarding advocacy, and enabling trade between the fan club members and Brand Z of which they become co-creators.

This is just an example. It's not exhaustive – it's simply a representation of the type of concept I envisage. I'm not proposing it replaces anything – just maybe adds to what is already happening perhaps…

I think it potentially requires adjusted payment systems, tracking systems, procedures and mindset. I don't think it's easy to get there, but I do feel this could be a way forward.

What's the first step? Well, I'd propose we start with one client and one agency agreeing on a general principle to begin with, and experiment in a small way with one campaign.

Pragmatically, a change to advocurrency will not happen overnight, and requires small iterative steps to happen, whilst learning all the time and fine tuning components as we go forward.

18. ARMIES OF FANATICS – a thought on how fans are a primary requirement for successful business

I remember when my son excitedly told me he had created an army and was desperate to show me.

I duly followed him into the lounge and saw his assembled army, split into two groups – one group on the higher level, apparently made up of the 'king' and helpers, and the other group as the 'troops'.

I find it interesting that such hierarchy seems obvious at an early age – perhaps it starts from looking up to the people who raise you.

A common theme I have been discussing over the last few years has been the need for companies to create armies of fanatics. Groups of people who adore your products and services to such an extent that they will defend and protect the brand reputation.

These groups do this so efficiently that one could argue the assignment of budget to nurture and facilitate such armies is the single best usage of budget in business.

Unlike my son's army, I perceive the need for these armies to be alongside rather than below any superior power. For the brave, your army of fanatics should be the people you follow rather than the other way round.

However – some companies have armies of fanatics who are certainly not followed and are very much sub-dominant to the holiest of holies. Let's take Apple for example.

You may remember the photo taken on 5th Avenue on the eve of the first iPad launch. That was the Cult of Mac.

To some it matters little what Apple release, there will always be people who will do almost anything to buy, use, defend, advocate and worship the brand.

Apple fanboys come in different strengths. I am a lightweight fanboy as I consider each product separately rather than blindly follow any release. However, other fanboys queue for four or five days outside a store to buy a $500 piece of kit, regardless of its capability.

Apple cares about their army in terms of ensuring adoption (via retail transaction), but they sure as hell don't listen to the army, let alone follow them.

I remember finding out that Real Madrid had a strong army of over 100,000 fanatics willing to pay €12/month to subscribe to fan club mobile services. Even without the dozens of extra games, wallpapers and apps, that is €14.5m per year… solely by servicing an army of fanatics with mobile phones.

I'm not talking about a customer base here. This isn't just about people within your CRM system. Don't be fooled if you just have an addressable 20 million customers. That's not necessarily an army of fanatics. How many would defend you, advocate you relentlessly and follow everything you do?

So, how does a company start building such an army?

Here are five pointers to begin with:

1. Access and assess the level of trust you have within your user

base

2. Determine the levels of value you provide and how that value could be scaled exponentially

3. Identify key influencers and ensure they are rewarded for what they do – including bringing more people into the army

4. Tirelessly continue to create more value whilst being guided by your army

5. Progressively give more of your company benefit to your army. Share the wins yet absorb the losses

I believe the companies that get this right have an extraordinary competitive advantage.

19. REFUELLING AT PEACETIME – a thought on why it is important to nurture fans once you have them

It seems like every day there is a new example of a marketing campaign that "went wrong".

At the time of writing the current examples include the twitter campaign from McDonald's restaurant that was 'hijacked' by the public who decided that the #MCDStories hashtag could be used for negative opinion rather than positive – thus turning the hashtag into a bashtag.

Elsewhere the Covent Garden Soup Company ran a competition that promised a prize of a £500,000 farm, but from the 200,000 entrants, none had the winning code so the prize wasn't given away. You may be surprised to know this didn't go down terribly well with the entrants – however the lawyers state the competition mechanic complied with regulation. That's ok then.

These are just two examples of daily stories that we all see in front of us, and are the result of the paradigm shift we are experiencing in the commercial, sociological, technological and communications landscape – a topic covered in the white paper I co-wrote on Brand Democratisation: http://thisfluidworld.com/branddemocratisation.pdf

One question I'm often asked is, "If these examples are claimed as having a negative impact, how come people are still (e.g.) queuing at McDonald's and/or buying Covent Garden soup?"

It's a fair question. After all, it is commonly thought the ultimate success a company can report is revenue, profit and/or share price. If the revenue, profit and/or share price remains in good shape, what exactly is the problem if these little campaign maladies are apparent?

To answer this I'd like you to imagine the competitive business landscape as a war zone.

In the old world, your army would consist of your staff. Your artillery would consist of your products and services.

In today's world, your army also consists of your customers and consumers. This is because of their empowerment enabled by the capability and affordability of technology, meaning they too can create and edit brands. They too can change the perceptions and opinions of others. Thus, your artillery now consists of their output also.

So, you have your combined army and often you have to go to war.

In the old world, your army of staff and artillery of products and services would be up against other armies of a similar structure.

In today's world, your asset is your army of staff, customers, and consumers, in addition to your combined artillery.

In the old world, at peacetime, you would just be fuelling your staff and polishing your artillery.

In today's world, at peacetime, you must also be fuelling the whole of your army, and polishing the extended artillery.

This is so you are prepared for when you go into battle.

Practically speaking this requires you to consider things like:

- identifying the levels of trust you have amongst your consumer/customer/user base
- creating resonant missions that people will believe in
- facilitating and promoting the work of fans
- etc…

These activities, amongst others, will better prepare you for the battles I speak of in the metaphor, which in real life look like:

- a new market entrant who is disrupting your organisation or market place
- a change in fashion that renders what you do less relevant
- a trend that alters the perceived value of what you create or deliver
- etc…

Sound familiar? These have always been common occurrences in every market place, yet now the risk is extended to competitive challenges that are non-organisational. Yes, the empowered public may be the cause of battle for a company today – and that, if nothing else, justifies the need to extend your army before those troops are aligned against you.

-

"All men can see these tactics whereby I conquer, but what none can see is the strategy out of which victory is evolved"

Sun Tzu – The Art of War

PART SEVEN: CITIZENSHIP

20. IT IS WITHIN – a thought on how to harness internal courage

I remember once walking off stage in Kiev where I had spoken in some detail about the necessity of courage when attempting to succeed. Someone approached me and asked whether I thought courage could be learned or whether you have to be born with it.

That is a good question.

My short answer was: "I think the challenge is less about learning courage and more about addressing the fears that create obstacles to what we desire to achieve."

Here is my longer answer:

Around 2500 years ago the Orphics had one of the first recognised religions to support the concept of personal heaven and hell. Damnation, redemption and salvation. Within.

Unlike earlier Greek religions that suggested a wide gulf between humans and Gods, the Orphics considered any believer to be able to find Godliness within their soul. Homer's humanised Gods, in contrast, were absolutely unattainable.

The Orphics said bodies were "the tomb of the soul" which successively imprisoned the soul through numerous birth cycles until final purification. It was thought that when a soul achieved full redemption it could dwell with the Gods evermore.

Incurable souls were condemned to lie in the "Slough" forever.

As it happens, I've visited Slough in the South of England and I can confirm it's a truly horrible place.

Anyway, despite the scarcity of historical evidence, (a few gold plates with writing on, buried in Italy and Crete with the remains of believers), Orphicism had a significant effect on all subsequent religions, including those that seem furthest removed from it.

Those enjoyable dinner party guests who have studied c.5th century B.C. enlightenment will confirm the main point being from Hippocrates in his treatise entitled 'On Airs, Waters and Places'[21].

"Nothing is more divine or more human than anything else, but all things are alike and all divine."

When I meet people around the world I sometimes drop in a few questions that tell me a great deal about them. These questions are exactly the same as I ask myself daily:

"What do you truly believe in?"

"Why do you do what you do?"

"What would you actually like to do?"

"What stops you from doing what you wish?"

It would seem these questions are about careers but actually they are about courage.

I like finding out what obstacles people perceive and whether they are capable of overcoming their fears to remove the obstacles in the way of success. You can tell a lot about people from whether they feel they are achieving what they desire.

Dan Gardner writes in the book 'Risk: The Science and Politics of Fear'[22] that our level of perceived risk is inversely proportional to our level of knowledge. In other words, when we know less about something our perceived risk is greater than when we know more.

The logic is that understanding means we can be rational and properly assess whether it is actually valid to be afraid of something. Unfortunately though, some of our deepest fears are irrational and not necessarily addressed with increased knowledge.

For instance, I recently had to hold the hand of a 60-year-old Turkish man on a flight to Istanbul because he was petrified of flying. Or at least that's what he said… I still have no idea why he wanted his leg rubbed.

When it comes down to it, our fear-based obstacles limit us from achieving our full potential.

Whilst one can learn whether the other side of an obstacle is attractive and safe, the root of our obstacle placement is based on our feeling of security.

The popular quote "feel the fear and do it anyway" is essentially a summary of the need to feel comfortable with the feeling of insecurity. This is not to say that feeling insecure is good. This is to say that feeling at ease with a lower level of security often opens the door to higher achievement.

I have found this to be true.

In my life I have felt extremely secure and extremely insecure at different times. Oddly, the most insecure I have felt was when I had the most traditional security. For example, when I had a 'proper' job, I always felt at high risk of everything being removed by a faceless board of directors.

As I am monumentally unemployable this was a realistic fear to have.

Personally I have no real idea of what my life will look like in 12 months and I embrace that feeling. This is because, ultimately, I have belief.

I believe in what I am doing to such an extent that nothing seems impossible. I am far beyond driven.

I have an extreme focus on what it is I would like to achieve and I am pretty sure I know how to get there.

If the road map is wrong, that's fine too. In fact if my aspirations change I will then have extreme focus on the new set.

As I have an 'open-arms' approach to changes in circumstance I am not remotely concerned if circumstances change.

Just as the Orphics said that (literally) every body contained the access path to divinity, I believe that (literally) every body contains the access path to achieving whatever is desired.

This is how I live, accountable and in control of my destiny.

From being given up at birth to experiencing times of hardship, loss, and constraint, I am living testament to the fact that anything you commit to and focus on is achievable.

Whilst the others wait to receive what they think they deserve, you have the absolute power to go out and get what it is you believe in.

It is within.

21. THIS IS YOUR HEART – a thought about acting upon your vision and purpose

The year is 1931 and a man called Michael Unterguggenberger has just been elected mayor of a small Austrian town named Wörgl. The events of the coming two years will create a story of vision, courage, and one of the most ugly, most pertinent examples of industries that would prefer to suffer than change. Due to that starkness, this story may well have been missing from your history class, even if you studied economics. However, this story is one of my favourite examples of how purpose, focus, and velocity, can produce the most miraculous results. Let us begin.

Born into a Tyrolean peasant family and having apprenticed himself to a master mechanic, Michael built a modest career whilst striving for social justice. His hometown, Wörgl, had grown rapidly in the early 1900s but was affected significantly by the financial crash of 1929. At the time, Michael was town councillor and eventually mayor two years later. Despite the numerous projects to re-build the town, the depression had driven a population of 4500 to include 1500 without a job and 200 families penniless.

Michael studied a book called "The Natural Order" by Silvio Gesell and theorised that the faltering economy was principally caused by the slow circulation of money. Money that increasingly moved from working people into the banks, without being re-circulated back into the market. His plan was to replace the common currency with "Certified Compensation Bills" that the public would be given to be used at their face value (1, 5 and 10 shillings). 32,000 such bills were printed and circulated.

Wörgl bills were designed to depreciate 1% of their nominal value monthly and the owner had to buy and place a stamp on the bill on the last day of the month, showing the devalued amount. Obviously as nobody wanted to essentially pay a premium (by losing value), bills were spent as fast as possible.

On the back of the bills this was printed:

"To all whom it may concern! Sluggishly circulating money has provoked an unprecedented trade depression and plunged millions into utter misery. Economically considered, the destruction of the world has started. – It is time, through determined and intelligent action, to endeavour to arrest the downward plunge of the trade machine and thereby to save mankind from fratricidal wars, chaos, and dissolution. Human beings live by exchanging their services. Sluggish circulation has largely stopped this exchange and thrown millions of willing workers out of employment. – We must therefore revive this exchange of services and by its means bring the unemployed back to the ranks of the producers. Such is the object of the labour certificate issued by the market town of Wörgl: it softens suffering's dread; it offers work and bread."

What a statement.

During the 13 months following, Michael initiated all the intended projects: new houses, a new bridge, even a ski jump. Six neighbouring villages copied the system to great effect and the French Prime Minister at the time, Edouard Daladier, made a special visit to see the "miracle of Wörgl".

Spin forward to January 1933 and Michael addressed a meeting with representatives from 170 towns and villages, all interested in adopting the concept.

The public was happy, employment was high, and poverty was virtually non-existent. People paid their taxes in advance enthusiastically and price increases (the first sign of inflation) didn't occur.

However, the Central Bank started to freak out due to its lack of control over the situation and decided to assert its monopoly rights by banning complementary currencies. Following a court case where the Austrian Supreme Court upheld the ban, it became a criminal offence to issue "emergency currency".

Wörgl quickly returned to 30% unemployment and social unrest spread like wildfire across Austria. Michael died in 1936 having watched his life's mission come into being, succeed brilliantly, then be stripped apart.

Two years later a chap called Hitler entered the scene and many people welcomed him as their economic and political saviour.

The rest, as they say, is history.

The thing that moves me about the story of Michael and Wörgl is the implementation of a vision into real life. There are so many good ideas around, so many interesting things that could be done, and so many idealists, but very few executors. To me it doesn't matter so much that the concept was ultimately outlawed (although it saddens me that many great concepts are killed at birth), the point is that it actually went to market.

I witness numerous people with new companies, new offerings, new concepts, all with kick-ass technology, fancy slogans, and cool haircuts but I rarely see robust go-to-market actions. It's almost as if we are living in perpetual concept stage.

Don't be fooled into thinking that Michael was only able to execute because he was mayor, in fact by 1912 he was elected representative for the union of Innsbruck Rail Engineers in the committee for personnel. He was seen as the person who represented the concerns of the workers against the capitalist interests of the railroad. His active campaigning at that time had a positive result for workers but yet a negative effect on his career progression because of it. His perseverance was due to the purpose that was in his heart. This was a guy who had found his path, focussed like hell, and applied his courage to move things forward.

I see a direct correlation between people who are following their heart and actual outcomes happening, versus people who are following only their head.

Maybe we should look within and ask, "Why am I really doing what I'm doing?" It is said that to truly know where your heart is, one must observe where our thoughts are when they wander… and I say that magical things can happen when we are properly playing from our heart. A blend of both is likely the best mix, but let's take the head thinking as a given, it's the heart piece I'm seeing mostly a lack of. But as Miles Davis said, "It takes a long time to play like yourself".

Michael, along with using your head, you played it from the heart. I salute you.

22. THE OPTION OF CIVILISATION – a thought on the parameters within which things are acceptable

During the year 1814 over 96,000 people visited Bethlam Royal Hospital (also known as Bedlam), to laugh at the mental patients. The visitors felt justified in doing so as the patients were considered to be "already destined for hell".

Many clever people commented on the definitions and causes of madness. One could cast blame on the education system, the Government, family upbringing or financial security, but it came to pass that mental illness was thought ultimately to be caused by moral weakness. Due to this, photography was seen as having a use in treatment and delusional patients were confronted with the image of their real selves. It was thought that issues of morality should be addressed with methods of moral awakening and reason.

Despite the development of thought over the last 200 years, our perception of life remains a product of our understanding of life in general, at any point in time.

Every generation generally believes its wisdom to be advanced. However, this perceived advancement is purely relative to prior generations' wisdom, so it follows that in numerous generations time our understanding of life will be far more advanced than now.

It is not that our current understanding is without merit, but instead that our current understanding is unlikely to be complete. This incompleteness is not solely horizontal across a timeline of history, but also vertical in terms of whom, at any point in time, has the most authentic, relevant and useful information to form the most complete understanding.

Let me explain.

We have challenges in society that must be addressed and in Great Britain it is the Government who has been elected to guide this. The understanding of life that they must apply can only be a combination of experience and thought (i.e. information) from the Members of Parliament, Civil Servants, and any other organisations or individuals they call upon for advice.

Thus the quality of Governmental decision is directly proportional to the authenticity, relevance and usefulness of Government's understanding that in turn is directly proportional to the authenticity, relevance and usefulness of the information provided to Government.

Many announcements we see that relate to present issues happening in society are based, understandably, on solving real-time challenges – and to these, everyone has an opinion. Following that phase, the announcements will move towards the wider and deeper issues. Again, these will be met with opposing opinions to which we are totally granted the right to have.

We are charged with having faith that those who will guide us forward are armed with the authentic, relevant and useful information from which to form an understanding and make the best quality decisions.

There are options available if that faith isn't within you and one of those options is to use the tools, platforms and channels we are armed with as citizens.

Maybe the collective voice of people can make a difference to how we move forward. After all, we have the ability to express ourselves more affordably than ever before.

Another option is to create or identify a political party that you do believe in, and either run for Parliament (if it is yours), or join/vote for it (if it is someone else's).

We all have options and we all have accountability for our happiness and contentment. However, something that is not an option in a civilised society is violent, criminal destruction.

I defend anyone's right to opinion and expression within the law, but when it manifests into ruining people's lives and turning once safe streets into war zones, any opinion becomes invalid.

If one wants things to change, one must use the facilities available and allowed.

All else is mindless thuggish bullying that I find deeply repelling and ridiculous, primarily in its immature ineffectiveness.

"When we show our respect for other living things, they respond with respect for us." Arapaho Proverb

PART EIGHT: IDEAS

23. EYEHOTEL – a thought on using privacy as a currency

I've come up with an idea for people to pay for hotel stays with their privacy, in a similar way to how we pay to use social networks by surrendering our privacy. I call it EyeHotel.

I'm keen on enabling people to realise the value of their private information, which is why I conceptualised a social experiment that could also explore whether *real* reality TV is more compelling than the manufactured versions we get on regular television.

The shell outline is: To provide the public with access to an EyeHotel room. Any member of the public can book a stay. There are no auditions.

An EyeHotel room costs £0.00 + privacy. This produces what I call Privacy as a Currency (PaaC).

Everything that happens in the EyeHotel room will be filmed with the permission of the resident.

This footage will be streamed 24 hours a day and 7 days a week and broadcast to the public on EyeHotel who can interact with people in the rooms and share the experience.

Hoteliers get paid at least the standard room rate and can remain anonymous if desired.

I have done quite a bit of background work on this already, covering the revenue streams (from premium subscription and product placement through to a new type of advertising called 'adver-rooms'), technical architecture, branding, marcoms, hotel outreach, legal necessities and operational requirements. I have the technology team lined up, there is a hotel in the pipeline and even the PR strategy is in place. I've been toying with the idea of actually pushing this forward, but for now, as an experiment, I have let this concept disperse into the market to see what happens.

I predict there are various outcomes of doing so:

1. Nothing – the idea sucks and it should be left alone
2. Others are inspired by the concept and make it happen independently of those who have assisted on this already
3. Someone wants to run with the project and would like me and the people I have worked with, to be involved in some way
4. The whole thing happens without any knowledge of my EyeHotel concept

I am fine with any of these four outcomes. If you choose option 3, please contact me.

24. PUBLIC URBAN BOUNDARY SYSTEMS – a thought on the potential of an analogue future

Everything is getting so augmented and virtual nowadays – soon we will be able to live much of our lives in a totally unreal place, commanding experiences at the touch of a button, viewing through walls and skin effortlessly.

It's tremendously exciting – but sometimes I wonder what will happen next. I mean, what will happen after everything is super virtual? What will follow? In my most bizarrely darkest hours I envisage people viewing IM and emails as fake signs of emotion, preferring instead to seal hand-written letters with wax stamps.

I envisage people paying a premium for mechanical, cog-based processors for even the simplest of tasks such as 'telling the time'.

I envisage a global society who communicate virtually in three or four dimensions, never needing to leave their 'pods' – but with the option to pay to walk down a 'Hi Street'. These areas are named as such because that is where you can say 'Hi' to a real person, i.e. one with flesh and blood.

Perhaps these toll roads, these 'Hi Streets', are encapsulated by areas that act as holding bays for people who would otherwise be greeting strangers…?

These could be called 'Public Urban Boundary Systems' or 'PUBS' for short. Eventually, if we push things far enough, we stand a good chance of ending up with reality.

25. SUPER OLYMPICS – a thought on using human enhancement and augmentation in sport

Super Olympics is a really simple concept. Basically, competitors can incorporate any type of modification to their bodies, up until the point where over 50% of their human body is un-human. In other words, not made up of their natural selves.

Let's start with some basic examples:

- A swimmer could wear a snorkel so they didn't have to take breaths
- A high jumper could use a pogo stick
- A long-distance runner could wear an oxygen tank

But this is just adding stuff on the outside. Let's widen our perspective:

- What if an archer could have a mechanical super-powered eye placed into their head, enabling increased visibility of aspects like wind direction and zoom-in control?
- How about a boxer with a robotised super-arm that delivered a knockout punch?

You can't say it's not fair. Anything goes.

If the technology was still not as super as one would need, I guess an extension of this would be to breed athletes with webbed feet and elongated arms? Genetic mutations would be all the rage and the vast range of imaginative technological implants would be a wonder to behold… if that's your 'thing'.

And I can guess your next question. What about drug enhancement?

Well, I'm not about to condone any illegal drug use, but the more rebellious amongst you may consider a scenario where an athlete could utilise any form of 'performance enhancer'. That's not what I'm suggesting at all. Lance Armstrong shouldn't expect a call to be the spokesperson just yet.

I'm just wondering how we can embrace the convergence of humans and technology in a good old-fashioned sporting event?

What other modifications do you see being viable? I have more but I've said enough.

26. THE EFFORT METRIC – a thought on prioritising effort alongside other standard business metrics

In the 1995 publication by John Kotter entitled "Leading Change: Why Transformation Efforts Fail"[23], his research from over 10 years showed that only 30% of change programmes are successful. Approaching almost 20 years on from then, McKinsey research shows that the figure is still around 30%.[24]

Kotter found that unsuccessful change management usually failed during at least one of the following eight phases:

1. Establishing a sense of urgency
2. Creating the guiding coalition
3. Developing a change vision
4. Communicating the vision for buy-in
5. Empowering broad-based action
6. Generating short-term wins
7. Never letting up
8. Incorporating changes into culture

Despite this insightful summary of where failure happens, I think there is another dimension at play. McKinsey's view is that the "Missing Management Metric" is the assessment of organisational health in relation to certain elements of "management practice needed to improve performance".

Notably their assessment of performance is determined ultimately in financial terms, as seen from their "five-step process that prioritizes management practices needed to improve performance" and as they say, "doing more doesn't add much value and involves disproportionate, not to mention wasted, effort."

From observation across all industry verticals, I've realised that Kotter's eight phases are consistently and exclusively viewed through a lens of financial priority.

Counterargument

There is one condition the common mindset depends on: the absolute requirement of a defined outcome with a financial target attached. This condition is valid in times that are stable and predictable, but bearing in mind the combination of macro economic crisis, slowing consumption and globalisation, alongside the increasing capability and affordability of technology, empowered citizens and democratised value chains; the current and future business environment is anything but stable and predictable.

Rather than defining an end result before the journey starts, the end result will be defined during, and because of, the journey. All of a sudden, change management isn't a one-off process but rather a constant management of change, and Kotter's eight phases no longer run as linear but parallel to each other.

Faced with this situation, I'd argue the common thinking achieves the absolute opposite of performance today. Instead, I'd suggest it breeds fear and chastity in innovation, limiting people taking chances and accelerating the probability of the brave getting fired. It ensures organisations chase figures rather than opportunity and it limits flexible growth. I believe that performance management in uncertain times requires a more valid "Missing Management Metric".

Introducing The Alternative Metric

I propose an alternative metric to supplement financial bias in modern business: Effort. This is because effort creates the opportunities as we exert it – mapping out our path during the journey. Here are five tangible elements needing to be prioritised, each with their own ways of measurement:

People: Identify those who are most comfortable with uncertainty in senior enough positions (or place them in such positions) so as not to suffocate the chances that could be taken. Also, identify or acquire people with this characteristic. The measurement of effort for this element should be via continual people auditing using a grid that plots volume of people with the 'comfort in uncertainty' characteristic against the level of seniority.

What good would look like is if there is a high volume of people with this characteristic in numerous senior positions. It's unfortunately sub-optimal if only junior staff have this characteristic.

Purpose: Be extraordinarily clear on what your purpose and vision is, so that every single person inside and outside your organisation knows the mission you are undertaking. The measurement of effort for this element should be via regular checking of how well the purpose is understood within the organisation and throughout external partners. This should be added to by a layer that checks how it is understood externally in public, through monitoring and ideally involvement in conversations outside the organisation.

What good would look like is if there was a) very high understanding and b) a close match between external interpretation and internal aspiration and definition.

Finance: Separate innovative, un-proven activities in the balance sheet. Placing the risk of not moving forward as the exact same cost as the funding of exploration. The measurement of effort for this element should be in two dimensions – a) of the finance team/director's willingness and proactivity in separating the balance sheet, assigning a tangible cost of risk through inactivity, and b) of the funding made available for the fourth priority coming up next.

What good would look like is if there was unarguable evidence of how the finances have been divided and maintained to be that way on an on-going basis, whilst continually assigning an amount for experimentation without formal targets.

Facilitation: Facilitate and reward those who are positively proactive in trying to push things forward whilst enabling them to initiate flexible un-promised projects. Remember not to link their activity to an expected outcome – however tempting. The measurement of effort for this element should be a) in the number of activities that facilitate momentum and b) in the regularity of rewarding the positive proactive people in a way that they feel valuably and relevantly rewarded (rather than something that is simply a token gesture).

What good would look like is if there was a high volume of facilitated activities with involved staff who feel permitted to experiment and rewarded in a way that made them want to strive to achieve more.

Learning: Learn from all outcomes regardless of what you may have once perceived as 'success'. A learning is as valuable either way. Feed this into iterative projects for constant adjustment at the speed of change. The measurement of effort for this element should be a) in the volume of learnings/insights as an output of each activity and b) in the volume of learnings that have been visibly fed into new efforts.

What good would look like is a direct link between output insights that feed into inputs.

There would be significant benefits of this approach – not least of which is the belief from colleagues that your organisation can flourish, so retaining the best staff will be easier, whilst collectively learning (in advance of your competitors) where the white space of opportunity is.

I believe that innovation would be properly fuelled in an agile and relevant way, and that this framework would legitimately sit alongside the common frameworks of financial aspiration.

I suggest this presents a desirable way forward where financial opportunity comes as a direct result of applied, prioritised and rewarded effort.

27. SYSTEM EFFECTIVE LIFESTYLE FILTERING – a thought on how technology could be used as an advanced concierge

System Effective Lifestyle Filtering, or SELF for short, is a concept I've been thinking about since I first used the Internet decades ago.

From time to time, people ask me what I look for in technology, or what cool stuff have I seen that really makes sense to me. I try and answer as honestly as possible, but if I were really pressed on it, I'd have to say there is still a significant divide between what I need and what is actually provided.

Here is what I need:

1. *Automation of repeatable tasks*, as I dislike repeating the same tasks when I have more productive things to do

2. *Efficiency of task completion*, when I do wish to carry out the tasks myself

3. *Subtlety of operation*, so that whatever automates or makes efficient, is invisible, silent and takes up little or no room in terms of space, and ideally using insignificant processing power

4. *Personalisation of how technology works for me*, meaning I don't need to learn a behaviour that is set by a developer, publisher or producer

5. *Compatibility of technology*, across any platform, meaning I can use anything I have in conjunction with anything else

6. *Intelligence of technology*, to learn based on insight, enabling permanent betterment and a reduction of insufficiency

I've been thinking about this for a long time, but after researching the industry over many years, and even spying the trends and developments, there is still a gap between how things work, and how I need them to work. Not only in technological deployments, but also in the mindset of many who bring solutions to market in general. The nearest thing is something like Tasker[25] and other variants – but I'm thinking about how we can extend that from apps only, into the real world, regardless of device and environment.

I've tried a multitude of solutions that claim to link together numerous parts of my digital existence. From Plaxo to MobileMe, from RoadSync to Google Apps.

Solutions that can integrate my calendar, email, contacts, notes so that everything is 'all in one place'.

I'm a massive fan of 'the cloud' and I'm attracted to things that allow me to access stuff on any machine and a screen.

I've played with scheduling apps; really cool GTD (Getting Things Done) tools like Omnifocus, services like Tungle and in the past you'd have rarely found a bigger advocate of Evernote than me.

I like things to be in sync and accessible, and I'd pay a significant premium if someone could guarantee me a permanent, strong, and fast Internet connection throughout the major cities in the world.

However, something is lacking.

I say this, aware that some may reply, "ah, but you haven't tried this," and I'm still unaware of anything that exists to truly answer my needs in this context.

I know for sure I'm imagining things that are platform independent, and agnostic in all ways. Made up of elements that require more psychology than technology in development.

Here are some trends in my life – and how SELF technology would work. Remember, I'm not talking about an application here – I'm talking about the glue that fits between random applications:

Between 8am and 8.25am, I am mostly available to take calls as I am driving.

SELF technology would configure my phone to ensure that the signal is strongest for me and alert the people who I've enabled to see I can take a call. Whispering to all parties "2 minutes remaining" at 8.23am.

Between 9.27am and 9.29am when working in London, I call up my colleague to find out where she is so we can meet and start work. She is often at a coffee shop 100 metres away from the station I arrive at. I always order fresh mint tea. She has a double espresso and water without ice.

SELF technology would look up my colleague's location and query whether we are meeting there or somewhere else. Confirming we shall meet, SELF orders (and pays for) my fresh mint tea as I turn the corner onto the street where the coffee shop is, so it's served as I arrive. At the same time, the ice machine knows it's her water being poured so doesn't dispense the ice into her cup, as she doesn't like it.

When I travel to Heathrow airport, I always pre-buy car parking (as it's cheaper), and always for the same car park.

SELF technology would sense my calendar and if it sees a Heathrow booking, it would reserve a parking space for me, alert me it had done so, then (if I press PAY), it would automatically pay the car park using my preferred bank details.

When I go on the tube to a meeting, I get out at the correct station (hopefully), then pretty much always open my calendar application to get the address, copy it, then open my maps application and hope there is sufficient signal to locate where I am in relation to where I am going.

SELF technology would automatically cache the map location so I can see it underground without signal. SELF triggers my device to vibrate when the correct tube station has been reached, then speaks to me a step-by-step guide of where I need to get to, regardless of signal. SELF alerts the receptionist of my arrival time and triggers a name badge to be generated, if applicable.

Most of the overland trains I get are packed full of people. Sometimes it's ok and I will crush in with everyone else. Other times, it's vital to get a seat (chair or floor, I don't care) as I have work to do which is harder standing up.

SELF technology alerts me to the parts of the train that have seating, as I'm walking down the platform, in real-time. Also, as stations are arrived at, SELF alerts me of newly available seating in other carriages.

These are just some random examples, but you can see that even in these simple versions, there are requirements that currently stretch the boundaries of what's available.

When smart fridges are commonplace, it will be SELF technology that you enable to link what you bought to your tendency to prefer a salad on a Monday, rather than cooked food.

SELF technology isn't an app. It's not a replacement for existing software.

It's not owned by the likes of Google or Apple – but yet it glues together parts of their native and developer utilities.

It's not exclusive to mobile (hence the fridge example).

It's as proficient and converged as you want it to be, or as basic as you demand.

If I were to be involved in the development of SELF technology, I would position it as free of charge – however, people can pay if they find it of value.

If they do, 70% goes to charity, 30% goes to the developers who enable SELF technology within their creations.

It would be a triple-win: developers have a new revenue stream, people have a totally compatible link between disparate systems, whilst charity aid is supported.

In closing, let's consider Christopher Kahler who once wrote for Mashable about "Why today's developers might be programming themselves out of tomorrow's jobs"[26] and argues that, "Eventually you won't need to have any technological knowledge in a world increasingly defined by technology", finally stating that, "The only remaining question is: Where are your ideas going to bubble up from?"

My answer is this: Hopefully from a SELF perspective. Hopefully from a mindset that stitches together tiny elements of our lives that currently require tolerance.

If you are reading this thinking, "this is exactly what I'm working on," I'd be delighted to connect with you.

28. NOISE: THE BUSINESS AND SOCIAL DISEASE – a thought on how we are affected by the volume of meaningless noise in life and business

This is an unusual paragraph. I'm curious as to how quickly you can find out what is so unusual about it. It looks so ordinary and plain that you would think nothing was wrong with it. In fact, nothing is wrong with it! It is highly unusual though. Study it, think about it, but you still may not find anything odd. If you work at it a bit you might just find out. Good luck!

Noise Destroys

The above puzzle may be familiar to those who often need to make decisions. There's an initial acceptance that a puzzle has been set, time needs to be spent studying the data and, finally, a decision needs to be made. However, distractions (like reading this sentence) can reduce the focus and provide more information to process. This isn't a trivial point as the fortune of companies rests solely on whether the decisions made turn out to be the right ones.

As a Social Technologist I assist others in understanding and capitalising on the effect that technology has on society and business. Evidently the need has never been greater. More than ever before, the volume of distraction is sky high, especially from connected technology. There have never been so many distractions competing for our attention, making decisions progressively harder.

In 2014, a single minute sees the emergence of 571 new websites, 278,000 new tweets, 204,000,000 emails, 2 million searches, 72 hours of uploaded video and 246,000,000 forum posts.

I'd wager that one of your several digital devices is competing with me right now for your attention. I'm envious; I don't have neon flashing lights or an icon that displays numbers, rising on a minute-by-minute basis.

I call these distractions 'noise'. The opposite of noise is 'signal', which is what really matters to us in a meaningful way. As we become more connected to each other, we find it harder to filter out the noise to find the signal.

I believe this is the primary reason for many of the negative aspects of modern life, including bad decision-making that often leads to business failure.

I'm convinced that as things progress there will be an increasing need to 'De-Noise'. This is the activity of filtering meaning out of distraction. Numerous companies and individuals will develop filters. Filters will be used as solutions to the most paradoxical problems, the toughest decisions and the hardest philosophical dilemmas.

The Business Disease

The 24/7 Wall Street analysis of "The Worst Business Decisions Of All Time" [27] makes compelling reading, yet there are many other theories as to how bad decisions happen. Today a popular view is that our brains are wired to be what Dan Ariely would call "Predictably Irrational"[28].

A few decades ago I was lucky enough to be one of the first students of what is now popularised (by people like Ariely) as Behavioural Economics. Even then we were able to show that all decision-making was affected by a collection of heuristics and biases. Since then we've had books like "Nudge"[29] by Richard H. Thaler and Cass R. Sunstein and "Freakonomics"[30] by Steven D. Levitt and Stephen J. Dubner that show hundreds of case studies supporting this modern theory.

Despite being very fashionable, this isn't the only perspective. One can find an alternative analysis within the 2009 book "Think Again – Why Good Leaders Make Bad Decisions"[31] by the Tuck School of Business professor, Sydney Finkelstein. He opens by stating, "Most leaders make bad decisions. Even great leaders can make bad decisions." His analysis crawls through 83 flawed decisions and finds there are four common "red flag" conditions that can lead to errors in judgement.

1. *Misleading experiences* – memories of what is thought to be a similar situation to the present one. For example, a new competitor has emerged in the marketplace and it reminds you of the time when you competed by lowering prices. Your subsequent success in your memory is firmly and forever linked to the price drop. Due to this, your strategic decisions are already biased toward lowering prices.

2. *Misleading pre-judgements* – where previous decisions or judgements influence your thinking. For example, if you tend to start a new job by immediately replacing the sales and marketing team, you are biased towards repeating the same behaviour, regardless of whether it is the most suitable thing to do in the present situation. It's just what you do.

3. *Inappropriate self-interests* – subconscious personal agenda that conflicts with the job in hand or the outcome of the business. For example, if a hidden driver is personal fame and recognition at almost any expense, this will affect the decisions that are made even without being fully aware that this agenda is being applied to other contexts.

4. *Inappropriate attachments* – loyalty and alliances that overrule rational or

logical decisions. For example, giving a particular team member more responsibility even if they didn't deserve it, or appointing a particular supplier even if they are not the best you could have chosen.

Finkelstein said: "Trust in our own judgement is so engrained it can make us ignore red flags that warn that a decision was flawed from the start. That's how bad decisions get made."

Finkelstein's theories are supported by looking at how I've observed decisions to be made – starting with information (i.e. inbound data from outside), into perception (i.e. how we view the information, sub-consciously guided by our heuristics and biases) and finally resulting with our decision (i.e. the chosen way forward).

In conclusion Finkelstein states that the antidote to this situation is in:

1. *Open-mindedness* – decision makers should be more open to new ideas and not afraid to look outside their comfort zones.

2. *Own up to mistakes* – being brave enough to admit when they're wrong.

3. *Awareness and acceptance of change* – In his own words: "Good leaders will get multiple sources of information and get honest feedback to make sure they are not missing or ignoring something that should be obvious."

Personally I believe the 3rd point is the most problematic as if you initially perceive information ineffectively, you are ultimately doomed in decision-making.

The reality is that it's becoming increasingly hard to perceive information effectively as there's so much information to process. However, paradoxically, we need to access more of the information to ensure we are aware of what is happening around us...

...and the distraction paradox grows by the minute.

The Social Disease

From a human perspective it has become apparent that distractive noise is impacting our lives regardless of whether we're at work or not. In any top ten list of unusual medical conditions, "Busy Lifestyle Syndrome"[32] is often mentioned.

Even a quick glance at the symptoms of Busy Lifestyle Syndrome will make you wonder whether it is really unusual or actually very common.

The primary outcome is losing track of the main thing we were thinking or doing. What was front-of-mind gets lost and we end up wrongly prioritising things that get us into all sorts of trouble.

The lead researcher on this, Dr. Alan Wade[33], says: "Forgetfulness is an ordinary part of getting older but anecdotal evidence suggests that it is now affecting people earlier in life as a result of busy work and home lives, and so-called 'information overload' from the various media channels we consume today."

This manifests as forgetting people's names, forgetting a task you were meant to carry out, forgetting the values you stand for, forgetting the main reason for doing something, or even repeating an activity you've actually already completed.

Researchers have speculated that the condition could be cured by a low dose of the drug memantine, that is used to treat Alzheimer's Disease. This makes sense if you consider that Alzheimer's is essentially when the brain can't convert short-term memories into long-term ones, meaning that memory itself dies away.

There's a worrying correlation between the volume of noise from connected technology and the increasing volume of relationship breakdowns, and you may have read recently that teenagers are reported to have never been more unhappy, despite being more connected digitally than ever. I'm pretty certain this information is linked to the 53% rise in the diagnoses of ADHD cases[34]. Perhaps there's even a correlation between these stats and the fact that by the time a child leaves primary school they will have witnessed around 8000 murders on television[35].

Are we becoming de-sensitised as a result of the information overload?

Are we losing track as a species of who and what we are?

What does this mean to society and future generations?

Back In Business

In the context of the business world though we are still dealing with humans making decisions. The business context does not remove the social context. We are all still members of society. Walking into an office building doesn't remove us from the increasing volume of noise in our lives. If anything it turns the dial up and makes the pressure of handling it even greater.

The behavioural economics that impact our decisions happen after the influx of noise. The pressure of the noise kicks in before we even get a chance to be biased.

Noise is the fuel of behavioural economics, accentuating our pre-set conditions, which we default to constantly. The more noise, the more our brain calls on our biases to 'help' us and, therefore, the more common it is to make flawed decisions.

I believe this is the primary reason why the life expectancy of a business is now nearer 15 years, reduced from around 75 years a century ago.

Noise is a business and social disease.

CONCLUSION

As I was compiling this book, I was concerned that my thoughts may become less relevant as time moves on, due to the rapid pace of change. For example, ideas like SELF are arguably becoming more common, and the online safety situation evolves by the day.

However, while some thoughts are moments in time, others are laced with hope and aspiration. Perhaps it is these that will carry forward best? For example, my thoughts on privacy, data and reason, are essentially dreams of a time where we start from purpose rather than profit. Elsewhere, my thoughts on fan clubs and loyal advocates are not specific to any moment in human history.

Ultimately my ambition in this book is to continue the thought expansion of you, the reader, and if you would like an on-going service of similar thought expansion, you can join my 'Thought Expansion Network' (also known as TEN). TEN offers continuous insight and opinion via video content, online masterclasses and live events.

More details can be found here: jonathanmacdonald.com/ten

If this is the first book of mine you've read, then you may also be interested in "*Business Poison – Diagnosing and treating the infectious poisons that determine your business success*". Business Poison was published at the turn of 2013/2014 and is a collection of observations of which infectious poisons run through the veins of organisations and what can be done about them, ultimately determining the fortune of all involved.

More details can be found here: jonathanmacdonald.com/books

APPENDIX

[1] FastCompany coverage of Princeton research (2013) http://www.fastcompany.com/3025273/fast-feed/study-facebook-will-lose-80-of-its-users-by-2017

[2] The Black Swan by Nassim Nicholas Taleb (2010) http://www.amazon.com/The-Black-Swan-Improbable-Robustness/dp/081297381X

[3] Tesco profit warning (2013) http://www.independent.ie/business/its-tough-surviving-at-the-top-as-tesco-profit-warning-shows-28957991.html

[4] Lego profit boost (2013) http://www.dw.de/lego-reports-sales-and-profit-boost/a-16616912

[5] Lego crowdsourcing diagnosed (2013): http://www.digitalsparkmarketing.com/innovation/crowdsourcing-design/

[6] End To The Lies by Jane's Addiction (2011) http://www.metrolyrics.com/end-to-the-lies-lyrics-janes-addiction.html

[7] The Starfish and the Spider: The Unstoppable Power of Leaderless Organizations by Ori Brafman and Rod Beckstrom (2008) http://www.starfishandspider.com/

[8] Agent Smith, The Matrix (1999) http://en.wikipedia.org/wiki/Agent_Smith

[9] Verner Vinge http://en.wikipedia.org/wiki/Vernor_Vinge

[10] The Coming Technological Singularity: How to Survive in the Post-Human Era by Vernor Vinge (1993) http://www-rohan.sdsu.edu/faculty/vinge/misc/singularity.html

[11] Primitive Expounder, Devoted to Theoretical and Practical Religion, Expounded in Its Primitive Purity, Excellence and Loveliness by R. Thornton & J. Billings (1845) http://books.google.co.uk/books?id=-sXhAAAAMAAJ

[12] Alan Turing http://en.wikipedia.org/wiki/Alan_Turing

[13] The Singularity Is Near by Ray Kurzweil (2005) http://en.wikipedia.org/wiki/The_Singularity_Is_Near

[14] "Superintelligence Does Not Imply Benevolence" by Mark Waser (2011): http://becominggaia.wordpress.com/2011/03/16/superintelligence-does-not-imply-benevolence-intelligence-vs-wisdom-1/

[15] trsst http://www.trsst.com/

[16] NSPCC http://www.nspcc.org.uk/

[17] EU Kids Online statistics (2013) http://www.lse.ac.uk/media@lse/research/EUKidsOnline/EU%20Kids%20III/PDFs/EUKidInforgraphic.pdf

[18] InternetSafety101 statistics (2013) http://www.internetsafety101.org/Predatorstatistics.htm

[19] BBC News (2013) http://www.bbc.co.uk/news/uk-23471982

[20] Taken from Vesalius in Zante, a poem by Edith Wharton (1902) http://www.readbookonline.net/readOnLine/3200/

[21] On Airs, Waters and Places by Hippocrates (400 B.C.E) http://classics.mit.edu/Hippocrates/airwatpl.html

[22] Risk by Dan Gardner (2008) http://www.amazon.com/Risk-The-Science-Politics-Fear/dp/1905264151

[23] Leading Change: Why Transformation Efforts Fail by John P. Kotter (1995) http://www.sykehusapoteket.no/Upload/Topplederprogrammet/Litteratur/2.1%20Leading%20Change%20-%20Why%20Transformation%20Efforts%20Fail%20by%20JP%20Kotter.pdf

[24] The Inconvenient Truth About Change Management by McKinsey (2000) http://www.mckinsey.com/App_Media/Reports/Financial_Services/The_Inconvenient_Truth_About_Change_Management.pdf

[25] Tasker http://tasker.dinglisch.net/

[26] Why today's developers might be programming themselves out of tomorrow's jobs by Christopher Kahler (2011) http://mashable.com/2011/05/13/developer-platforms-jobs/

[27] The Worst Business Decisions Of All Time by 24/7 Wall Street (2012) http://247wallst.com/special-report/2012/10/17/the-worst-business-decisions-of-all-time/

[28] Predictably Irrational by Dan Ariely (2010) http://www.amazon.com/Predictably-Irrational-Revised-Expanded-Edition/dp/0061353248

[29] Nudge by Richard H. Thaler & Cass R. Sunstein (2009) http://www.amazon.com/Nudge-Improving-Decisions-Health-Happiness/dp/014311526X/ref=pd_rhf_dp_s_cp_2?ie=UTF8&refRID=0TT73J7SDW6F5BFX93WW

[30] Freakonomics by Steven D. Levitt & Stephen J. Dubner (2009) http://www.amazon.com/Freakonomics-Economist-Explores-Hidden-Everything/dp/0060731338

[31] Think Again: Why Good Leaders Make Bad Decisions and How to Keep it From Happening to You by Sydney Finkelstein (2008) http://www.amazon.com/Think-Again-Leaders-Decisions-Happening/dp/1422126129

[32] Busy Lifestyle Syndrome as reported at news.com.au (2012) http://www.news.com.au/lifestyle/health/why-are-we-so-forgetful-again/story-fneuz9ev-1226544547362

[33] Dr. Alan Wade from CPS Research http://www.cpsresearch.co.uk/who-we-are/directors

[34] 53% rise in the diagnoses of ADHD as reported by NY Daily News (2013) http://www.nydailynews.com/life-style/health/adhd-diagnoses-jump-53-decade-cdc-article-1.1304626

[35] ParentsTV.org statistics (2002) http://www.parentstv.org/ptc/publications/reports/stateindustryviolence/main.asp

Made in the USA
Charleston, SC
27 February 2017